Collecting
Natural Objects

Collecting
Natural Objects

JOAN RENDELL

CASTLE BOOKS
Distributed to the trade by Book Sales Inc.,
110 Enterprise Avenue, Secaucus, New Jersey

Printed in Great Britain

Contents

Illustrations

(*Photographs by Colin Peacock; drawings by Ann Thomson*)

To Zeus, my constant collecting companion,
who enjoys the open air life as much as I do

Introduction

There is a little bit of the magpie in everyone. Some have the instinct more fully developed than others, but there are few people who have not, at one time or another, picked up an intriguingly marked stone or a curiously shaped piece of wood, a dainty shell, or other examples of the trifles created by nature for a serious purpose and then left lying around on beach or in woodland for the pleasure of any observant member of the human race. But once carried home, what can be done with such treasure trove? Often the souvenirs are just thrown away; indeed, we may feel slightly ashamed of holding on to 'childish rubbish!'

That, then, is where this book sets out to help. Don't throw away all those bits and pieces—a spontaneous delight in the beauty of a feather, the smoothness of a pebble, the colour of a stone, the interest of all sorts of bric-à-brac, can be turned to lasting pleasure by starting a more selective hobby, with some purpose. For instance, several attractively coloured bits of stone and rock picked up from a beach, or from an old mine, can be the nucleus of a rock and mineral collection, with all the interest of arranging, adding to, and classifying the pieces, of meeting other people with a similar interest, and having something to show to friends and family. Or, if you prefer making things, you may be able to turn your finds into unusual and attractive ornaments, for your home or to wear. In either case you will be creating a relaxing hobby which will take you into the open air when the weather is good, and provide an interest at home in the winter.

You may succumb first to the sheer aesthetic appeal of strangely shaped pieces of driftwood, or a desire to study the structure of leaves or to capture the fragile beauty of spiders' webs. Wherever you start, you are off on a journey of discovery, always opening fresh windows on life. There is almost no end to the bounty which nature leaves lying around: make the most of it—take and use gifts so freely offered.

CHAPTER ONE

Starting a Collection

It is seldom realised just how many natural objects *can* be collected, and how many can lead on to interesting hobbies. All or any of the following may be considered: flowers, grasses, ferns, lichens, fungi, mosses, seed pods and cones, driftwood, samples of wood, feathers, spiders' webs (yes, you can actually collect them!), seedlings to be grown into miniature trees, sheep's wool from fences and hedges, sand, shells, seaweeds, minerals, rocks, fossils and pebbles. Even a few fruit stones are worth keeping as the start of a collection of indoor fruit trees.

In starting a collection, personal circumstances must be taken into account. The person who seldom if ever visits a beach will obviously not choose to collect sea shells. If one is physically unable to partake in strenuous activities, then the collecting of minerals or fossils is not advisable, as the search for them entails a good deal of walking and scrambling about over rough terrain. People who are 'good with their fingers' will probably want to collect something they can use artistically, thus combining a simple craft with the interest of collecting its materials. The neglecter of house plants is unlikely to succeed with miniature trees, and the apartment dweller may not have the space required for the

11

effective display of a collection of driftwood.

Whatever you choose to collect, you will first need a little basic equipment. This can be very simple and cost practically nothing; on the other hand specially designed equipment is available for some of the better-known collecting hobbies, and may well be worth buying as your collection becomes established or your interest develops. But you will not want to burden yourself with too much equipment on field trips, when everything you carry tends to get heavier and heavier.

Most important of all, you will need a pair of heavy shoes (not rubber-soled for wet surfaces) or if you are seeking items on the seashore, by river banks, or in wet woods a pair of rubber boots —the type with well-cleated soles.

Let us examine some of the things that will help in the assembling of each of the collections listed at the beginning of this chapter. For carrying out various crafts at home further equipment may be necessary, but that will be dealt with under the appropriate chapter headings.

Flowers, grasses, ferns

In the actual gathering of plants for a really good collection of pressed flowers, a metal box with a firmly fitting lid is all that is needed. An airtight plastic lunch-box would serve the purpose, but metal is preferable as it is less likely to be crushed. It is possible to buy specially made botanists' collecting boxes, with a strap for slinging over the shoulder. This is an advantage in keeping hands free, especially if your search for plants takes you into difficult locations as on cliffs or rough land. This special plant carrier is called a botanical vasculum and can be obtained in various sizes, in galvanised or aluminum. Although the aluminum variety is a little more expensive it is a wise investment as aluminum deflects heat and therefore the interior of the container remains cool; black galvanised absorbs heat and does not keep specimens so fresh. (You will find details of suppliers of botanical equipment on page 125.)

You may care to add a small trowel to your field equipment if you want to collect complete plants, roots and all; miniature trowels used for indoor gardening are obtainable quite cheaply at chain stores or gardening shops. But remember that rare plants should *never* be uprooted and that only one specimen of the flower and/or leaf should be taken. A great many varieties of wild plants are now almost extinct, to which uprooting has contributed— even if the main causes are changing farming methods and industrial development. It is at any rate the duty of the serious collector to do all in his or her power to conserve and not destroy wild plants.

A notebook is important for collectors in the field, for jotting down details of where and when a specimen was found and any special points of interest which might otherwise be forgotten by the time you reach home.

Lichens, fungi, mosses
Here again the metal tin or vasculum is your main item, plus the trowel, which will be most useful for digging out the type of fungus that has a short thick base or grows close to the ground. A blunt-ended knife is necessary for removing some lichens from tree trunks and branches—an old kitchen knife or palette knife will serve the purpose admirably. A small geological hammer and cold chisel are also handy when lichens on rocks cannot be removed with a knife: you will then be able to take samples still adhering to the stone. For fungi a compartmented box is desirable, as otherwise the specimens roll about and damage each other. An egg box, or a piece cut from one of the cardboard layers that are placed between eggs when they are packed in quantity, could be put in the collecting box to hold specimens safely, but first of all line each compartment with moss. The experts wrap each specimen in waxed paper.

Small plastic bags fastened with elastic bands are the most

convenient way of carrying moss specimens. (But don't leave them about—plastic bags are today the bane of farmers' lives: they are indestructible by natural processes so remain a blot on the landscape for ever, and can also be most dangerous to animals. Just as plastic will not disintegrate in the open air neither will it disintegrate in an animal's stomach, but will cause death.)

Seed pods and cones
Ordinary paper bags can be used for carrying these. A pair of pruning shears or heavy scissors will often be necessary.

Driftwood
No special equipment is needed for the collection of driftwood, apart from some sort of carrier; anything from a small basket to a back pack can be useful.

Samples of wood
A small saw for cutting thin slices of wood from a selected branch is all that is required. Some collectors include a tape-measure or other type of rule to ensure that they get samples of more or less uniform circumference.

Feathers
These cannot always be found by just going out to look for them. At any rate, there are no problems about getting them home!

Spiders' webs
To collect these ephemeral things you will require some strong, black matt paper (about 15 cents a sheet at most stationers) and an aerosol can of white paint. How to use the paper and paint will be explained in a later chapter.

Seedlings
A trowel and a supply of small plastic bags are all you need in the field.

Seaweeds
A metal box (leakproof!) or plastic box in which the specimens can be laid flat is better than a plastic bag. The tougher specimens such as bladder-wort can stand the bag treatment, but dainty corallines are fragile and should be laid in the collecting box on a bed of folded newspaper, with sheets of paper between each specimen so that they do not become tangled. Some collectors float delicate specimens on to a sheet of thin glass such as is used in protecting photographic transparencies, and then allow them to dry on the glass and remain there permanently.

Sheep's wool
Quite a lot of this can be crammed into a large plastic food bag, much more, in fact, than you are likely to find on any one expedition. Do not attempt to clean the wool until you get it home.

Sand
You will not want to collect more than a few ounces of each variety and for this a small scoop, obtainable for a few cents at a chain store, plus a good supply of small plastic bags and some elastic bands or pliable wire twists to secure them are the main items needed. If you are collecting samples from different parts of a beach or from several beaches then the exact location of each specimen should be marked on a small self-adhesive label stuck on the outside of each bag.

Shells
Matchboxes lined with cotton for small specimens, small plastic bags for larger and tougher specimens (one shell only to a bag) and the ever-useful notebook are basic equipment. A pocket lens is useful. More ambitious collectors may like to have a net, with

small mesh and a long (preferably extending) handle, and a trowel or small spade.

Rocks, minerals, fossils

For collecting these a little outlay on equipment is absolutely essential. A geological hammer and cold chisel are basic needs and there is really no substitute. Cheap tools are a poor investment as they will not stand up to the hardness of the materials on which they are to be used, whereas proper geological tools will last a lifetime. Choose the weight of hammer suited to you; a 2lb one is average, but you may care to invest also in a really big hammer for those occasions when you do not have to carry your equipment a long way—but be sure that you are strong enough to wield it! The chisel may vary in size from $\frac{1}{4}$in to 1in; it is advisable to have one large and one small one. Prices for suitable hammers start at about $5·00, and chisels at about $2·00.

Also essential is a soft knapsack (the non-frame variety). Individual preference is important here but ex-army knapsacks are strongly recommended. They are obtainable at shops selling camping or surplus army equipment and cost about $4·00 to $9·00 (nylon) and $2·00 to $7·00 (canvas), according to size and condition. A pair of gardening or household gloves is a great help, even if you feel your hands are tough. A magnifying glass for examining specimens in the field, lots of newspaper for wrapping them, a few matchboxes lined with cotton wool for small or delicate specimens and the ever-useful plastic bags and notebook are also 'musts' for rocks, minerals or fossils. Some collectors like to add what is known as a 'wrecking bar' or 'wrecking hook' to their equipment, using it for prising nodules from clay and so on; others favour a strong knife or a small mason's trowel for this purpose. The choice is a personal one and you can get by without these; one really important thing, however, that the amateur rock hunter often overlooks is a pair of goggles to protect the eyes from flying fragments when breaking stones. It is most unwise to try to

16

do without them. Most cycle shops or garages that service motor cycles stock goggles in a wide price range.

The above list gives just the essential requirements: other equipment can be added as desired. You will find, for instance that magnifying glass, notebook and pencil and adhesive labels are useful on *all* collecting expeditions. A clear large-scale map is a great boon if you are covering country which is unfamiliar to you.

CHAPTER TWO

When to Collect

Contrary to what many people think, the collecting of natural objects can be an all-the-year-round occupation; there is no need at all for it to be confined to the summer months when the great outdoors is at its most enticing.

Spring and autumn are profitable times for collecting most of the things listed in this book; in fact, they are often better than the summer—beaches are less crowded, roads are not so busy, and some of the items you may be interested in are at their best. Winter, too, can yield plenty of treasures, and has its own advantages. When trees are bare of foliage and undergrowth has died down there are greater opportunities for discovery; fields are often empty of cattle and as there are few growing crops farmers are less likely to object to people walking through their fields in search of specimens. Most farmers and landowners are co-operative if you seek permission and satisfy them that you will cause no damage, but remember that damage includes breaking off large branches of trees, cutting fences or damaging them in any way, and scattering stones or other debris on the pastures or fields.

In collecting **flowers, grasses** and **ferns** you will naturally have to take them in season, but spring, summer *and* autumn can be busy times, as you may wish to collect leaves and seeds as well as just the flowers. This gives you a life history of the species and is more interesting than going for flowers alone. Moreover, you have a chance to learn about the habitat; each time you visit your particular plant, there is another nearby for you to observe and add to your collection. An all-season study of ferns and grasses is rewarding in the same way. It is better, by the way, not to pick flowers when the summer sun is full on them; morning and evening are far better times for collecting—the flowers will look fresher when pressed if they are not gathered in the heat.

You will probably want to gather branches of leaves for preserving in glycerine, and if you intend to use these in flower arrangements it is advantageous to gather sprays at different times of the year. Young beech leaves picked in late May or early June turn a light brown when given the glycerine treatment; those picked later in the year come out darker and darker; and the very last of the green leaves, picked just before they start to turn yellow, go a very dark brown indeed, and have a completely different texture from those glycerined in spring or early summer.

If you are interested in flora you may like to see how many different kinds of shoots you can collect for the making of simple baskets and other items. A later chapter discusses which species are suitable for this work, and there is really quite a variety. Shoots should be gathered between October and March, when the sap is at its lowest.

Fungi and **lichens** are really one and the same thing, but in speaking of fungi for the purpose of this book we are referring to the fleshy types, the 'toadstools' and the plate-like growths found on the trunks and branches of dead or dying trees. For the collecting of fungi late summer and early autumn are best, though some varieties may be taken earlier. Many species, when gathered, change colour after a certain length of time, and in order to facilitate identification the whole fruit body should be brought

19

A selection of natural objects

home intact. Some species should be completely dug up, and those that grow out of wood should be cut away on the piece of wood or bark to which they adhere. Details recorded in your notebook on site should include a note on the habitat, and on smell, colour, texture—any feature of the fungus, in fact, that might change after it has been gathered.

It is best to collect lichens from trees when the branches are bare of leaves: they are almost invisible when the verdure is thick. Lichen growing on stones can either be prised off by inserting a sharp-pointed knife beneath the growth and lifting gently, or where this is more than usually difficult take the stone as well (if it is not too big).

Seed pods and **cones** are also usually a product of late summer. It is important to gather cones when they are young and still tightly closed, for in this condition they will last in good trim almost indefinitely. When they have become more mature they act as the countryman's weatherglass, opening and closing their scales according to changes in temperature and humidity. Once fully open it is impossible to close them again, so only take wide-open specimens if you require them that way for some decorative purpose.

If it is **driftwood** you are seeking, then you will get your greatest reward if you make your way to a beach after a storm and when the wind is blowing in off the sea. In these conditions there will usually be a few interesting specimens above the tide-line; on a much-visited beach during the summer all the best pieces are soon picked up, so this is the least profitable time for collecting. The heavier, chunkier pieces will be found caught up in rocks; lighter stuff gets washed up the beach more easily. Driftwood has become very popular for use in flower arrangements, or as an ornament in its own right, and local inhabitants are usually quick off the mark after a storm, so even out of season it is advisable to get to the beach in the early morning if possible, provided of course that the tide is right. River banks and lake shores can offer driftwood at any time of the year.

Samples of wood are best taken in winter when there are no leaves to obscure likely looking branches, and also when the wood is dry. Sawmills or local lumber yards may allow you to look round their yards for fragments or miniature slices. (But sawmills must never be ventured into without permission from the management or person in charge, and supervision, if offered or insisted upon, must be accepted in the interests of safety for all concerned.)

The methodical collector of **feathers** will do well to read up beforehand the details of when certain species moult and are likely to cast feathers, and also, of course, about their habitat if in doubt. It would be no good looking, even at the right time of year, for an oyster-catcher's feather in an inland district, or for a robin's feather on the beach!

But **sheep's wool** you may find at almost any time of the year. It tangles in barbed-wire fences, prickly bushes and low branches; it does not deteriorate much with the onslaught of bad weather conditions and usually remains in good condition for quite a long time. The misty mornings of late August or September are the time for **spider's webs,** although they can be located during most of the milder months of the year. But these misty-morning webs, with minute drops of water adhering to them, make stronger designs on the paper when collected and often hang in pretty curves through the weight of the moisture.

The collector of **seedlings** for growing into miniature trees should gather specimens preferably in the early spring when the sap is beginning to rise. A lot depends, however, on the country, or part of the country, in which one lives or intends to collect. It is best to watch the seedling you propose to adopt and try to judge the right moment for digging up and potting, according to the climate. This is something which can only be learnt by experience. If you have already grown seedlings from fruit stones it is as well to remember that flowering plants such as peaches or plums are most satisfactorily re-potted just after flowering and before the leaves open. Some growers of bonsai, Japanese miniature trees, advocate the digging up of specimens in the winter, when the trees are dormant. But here again, it is wise to read up the subject before making your selection.

Sand and **shells** can be gathered at any time of year. Search for your **seaweeds** when the tide is going out, for the specimens left stranded will be nice and fresh. Seaweed which has dried hard in the sun is useless for mounted specimens, although dry, twisted pieces are often very useful for flower arrangements, especially if you happen to be doing one with a marine theme. Storms wash up rarer varieties of seaweed, torn from the ocean bed, so the winter often produces the best finds.

Minerals, rocks, pebbles and **fossils** are other items which can be collected all the year round. But again winter is in fact a good time as there is less vegetation and if there is no snow specimens can more easily be seen. Wet weather is also useful as the colours of rocks and minerals show up more brightly. Look for pebbles at the edge of the sea just as the tide is receding, rather than higher up the beach where they have had a chance to dry. If collecting from a raised beach or above the water line—and often the best finds are made here—choose a damp day or go after a shower of rain. Record in your notebook whether the pebbles are taken from above or below high-water mark; and if from the water's edge then note down the state of the tide.

The best time for searching for fossils is after the winter. Snow and rain will have eroded the earth exposing fossils in the ground and shifting rocks containing specimens. In gravel and sand quarries too, especially those that are no longer worked, storms will wash away loose rock and gravel and may bring fresh fossils to light.

CHAPTER THREE

Where to Collect

PLANT MATERIAL

Every collector has his or her favorite spot for obtaining certain things. It might be a particular beach, a stretch of desert, a forest or a back road which is especially profitable. But don't get conservative: sometimes the most unexpected things appear in the most unlikely locations.

Flowers, for instance, are not the prerogative of woods or hedges. Deserts, cliffs, even stony mountains and uninviting swamps and mudflats have their own types of plants; some may be difficult to find but are worth searching for. Even the occasional plant collector will of course need a *Flora,* a book dealing with the plant life of the country or district, with which to identify plants and to discover where to find particular species, whether in woods, hedgerows, open country, on chalky or sandy soil, and so on.

The fern collector will obviously get the best haul in shady, moist places, but scrubland and mountains and old walls attract certain species, and here again the *Flora* will be of use. Bear in mind that most ferns do not like limestone and although they may be found in limestone areas they are usually very poor specimens, stunted and ill-nourished. People who live in the southern hemisphere, where ferns often grow larger than some of the trees, may smile at the idea of collecting ferns. But even in the famous tree-fern forest of New Zealand there are smaller, humbler species growing in the shade of their big relatives. Many cities have botanical gardens with collections of growing ferns of all types and they are well worth a visit by those interested in the subject. Advice and information will usually be readily given by experts at these establishments.

The woods are also a fruitful hunting-ground for the fungi, lichen and moss enthusiast, but are again by no means the only location suitable for exploration and collecting forays. Old stone walls often prove a profitable source of specimens, and stones lying on the ground will sometimes be found to be harbouring scaly lichen growths which often form interesting patterns. Dead trees are occasionally 'decorated' with the type of fungus which looks like a plate or saucer growing out of the trunk or branches of the tree. Some lichens flourish best in exposed, damp and windswept locations and this is particularly true of the species known as 'Spanish moss', resembling a beard or long hair hanging down from a branch.

Fungi and moss inhabit areas around streams but they also appear in meadows, hedges and old walls. In northern Scandinavia the reindeer feed with relish on the sphagnum mosses that grow freely on the tundra there. Many garden shops sell packs of compressed sphagnum moss, but the finest is sold in the country markets of Sweden and Finland, where it is a special species; botanically it is really a form of lichen. Some of the most brilliantly green mosses grow in swampland and great care must be taken in collecting these because in some swamps there may be quick-sand, so always test ground before stepping on it and if in any doubt about its stability *do not* venture on to it.

The moss collector might like also to add liverworts to his collection as these unobtrusive moss-like plants grow in the moist conditions which so many mosses enjoy, and some flourish on damp earth, on the bark of trees (especially if it is inclined to be

25

rotten) and even in running streams. The liverworts are very green and attractive little plants and usually press well for a collection. The herbarium at Kew Gardens, London, lists over 8,500 species of liverwort, so there is plenty of scope for the amateur botanist who fancies specialising in these.

Even in a town it is possible to collect seed pods and cones (which are also, of course, containers for seeds). Conifer cones, especially, vary a great deal and make an interesting and easy-to-preserve collection. The ornamental trees and shrubs in public parks or in friends' yards are quite as likely to provide you with new specimens as, for instance, a dense forest in the Rocky Mountains. Look on the ground under such cone-bearing trees for specimens and choose the young ones that have not yet opened their scales.

DRIFTWOOD

The collector of driftwood may be gathering spoils for use in flower arranging, for trimming and polishing to make pieces of natural wood sculpture, or merely for its sheer beauty of form or exquisite patina. Obviously if specimens from foreign lands are wanted the beach is the place to look. Search among the rocks, where pieces are often stranded, as well as along the tide-line. On non-rocky beaches the point reached by the highest tides is where driftwood may have been deposited, so get back from the water's edge (which is unlikely to yield much anyway) and poke among the debris higher up the beach. Do not be put off by the uninviting conglomeration of empty plastic containers, old beach shoes, tangled seaweed and other rubbish washed up by the tide. If you turn it over you may find that it is concealing some superb pieces of driftwood. One collector I know always uses a garden rake for that purpose.

Wood which has been in the sea for a long time is usually bleached to an attractive grey shade by the combined action of sun and salt water, and it is this quality which appeals to many people. But the beach is not the only place where driftwood may be gathered. Freshwater driftwood, often beautifully polished, can be found on river banks and lake shores. Some of my own most interesting pieces, however, have been found miles from water— in hedges, in woods, or even swamps. When land is cleared for building lots as it frequently is these days, the roots of maple, oak and other hardwoods are dug out and often left to be burnt or thrown away. It is here that some specially good finds can be made, and although the specimens may not at first look very interesting, they can be prepared in such a way that they become really artistic (we will deal with this in a later chapter). Look also in high open places for wood weathered by sun, wind, rain and snow which, having been exposed for years in the open, has developed a soft gray color which is most attractive. Slightly burnt branches found in areas that have suffered forest fires or brush fires can be polished to resemble ebony.

SEAWEEDS, SANDS AND SHELLS

It seems superfluous to tell anyone where to look for seaweeds— obviously the seashore is the only place! But specimens which have been stranded for a long time above the average high-water mark are often bleached to a colour quite different from their natural one and are therefore difficult to identify. What may at first appear to be an unusual species can easily turn out to be quite a common one.

When we think of sand we naturally think of the seashore again, but although beaches do provide a great variety of sands one can still build up a fine collection without ever going near the sea. Lake shores and river banks are ideal places from which to obtain samples. For instance, in France a curious type of brown sand, unlike any other elsewhere, is found in the forest near Bordeaux. In Wisconsin, a certain river bank yields a bright canary-yellow sand, and a stream at Manaccan in Cornwall, England, yields a black sand. And, of course, gravel pits everywhere produce fine sand as well as coarser gravel. But the best places to see a magnificent variety of sands are the deserts of the Southwest, called painted because of their colorful sands.

Black sand is also found on the beach at Ostia, near Rome, and people used to roll in it thinking that it had active curative powers. Along the Atlantic coast of Florida, there are coral beaches where the sand is composed almost entirely of minute pieces of broken coral; and at Svolvaer in the Lofoten Islands, off Norway, is a beach where the sand is made up of minute shells and foramins too tiny to be seen with the naked eye. You can, if you wish, collect unusual sands from round the world, but you do not in fact have to travel very far from home to discover sands of widely differing variety, texture and color.

As with sands, so with shells. Some shell collectors specialise in land snails and never bother with the shells of sea creatures, but generally the shell collector is most likely to have started off by being attracted by some curious sea shell, and most collections are in fact gleaned from the seashore, or, if one is interested in skin diving, from the sea bed. I remember being told when a child that all shells retain the rhythm of swirling water in their formation and it is surprising how a closer study of different types of shell convinces one of this.

Selling shells is now big business and most coastal resorts have shops which stock wide selections of tropical and other shells not found in the area, varying in size from large abalones to small cowries. This is the easy way to build up a collection, but also the most expensive way, and there is never the same satisfaction in a bought specimen as there is in one you have found for yourself.

The most productive shell area in the western hemisphere (from the point of view of range and size of specimens) is Florida's Sanibel Island and Captive Island. Occasionally, after a storm, rows of shells lie two to three feet deep on the beach of Sanibel

Polished driftwood
(Photographed by courtesy
of R. H. Cory)

Island. The famous abalone comes from the Californian coast, where it is protected by law against over-collection. The Algarve coast of Portugal is well known for its many varieties, as are parts of the Costa del Sol in Spain, now so popular with vacationers. The most exotic shells can be found in the South Sea Island paradises, but there are hundreds of very beautiful, if less bizarre, specimens to be found around the coasts of the United States. For those who seldom visit the ocean, or prefer to specialise in land and/or freshwater shells, there is plenty of scope in or near ponds or lakes, slow-flowing rivers, hedges, old walls and many other places. Land snails are nocturnal creatures, and wandering around the yard after dark, wielding a flashlight, can often be a very rewarding exercise on a warm night.

MINERALS AND FOSSILS

The great advantage of mineralogy as a hobby is that the collecting of minerals, unlike the collecting of other natural objects, yields much the same results the world over. True, you will not find emeralds in the USA, but many of the things you will find in America can also be found in, for instance, Australia. You will recognise amethyst when you find it in Maine or North Carolina and you will recognise it when you find it in Brazil—it is just as simple as that!

Anywhere where the ground has been eroded, excavated or cut away is a likely hunting area for rock or mineral specimens. Beaches, cliffs, caves, quarries, mine dumps, road workings, deserts, river banks, river beds and lake shores can all reveal specimens for the careful searcher. Although results may not often be spectacular, exciting finds *can* sometimes occur. When starting work on any area weigh up the scene and the possibilities before you begin digging or cracking stones. This will save a good deal of time and minimise the risk of disappointment. For instance, you may be visiting an old disused quarry or mine. Searching

Seaweed and shells

at the base of the workings will not be very productive; it has all been picked over many times before and you could spend hours there and come away empty-handed. But look about a bit; quite possibly the stones in one area have piled up in a not-very-steep slope and trickling down that slope is a little stream. If you scramble up the slope (making sure, of course, that it is safe to do so) and when nearly at the top start raking around in the bed of the stream, you may well be rewarded with some nice crystals of amethyst or smoky quartz, just to name two possibilities. In other words, let the stream do the work: it is constantly flowing, constantly eroding, washing out specimens that can then be found by the discerning searcher. We have already seen that rocks and minerals show up better when wet, so you will spot them more easily in the bed of the stream. Nearly always, this careful observation of the site will pay dividends, so never be in too much of a hurry to commence operations.

Anyone who spends a little while in the basaltic rock formations of the West can pick up a specimen of chalcedony or agate. When polished smooth and held up to the light, it will be seen to be semi-transparent. The common minerals vary depending on the geological history of your area. As you learn about rock formations you can travel around the country in search of different minerals.

Working quarries often reward the collector with good specimens. With modern methods of working, the rock faces are not 'cleaned up' as they used to be when quarrying was a manual process, and so falls of rock can and do occur from time to time. Permission has to be sought before entry, and some quarries are not open to the public at all, probably because conditions are too dangerous, so a refusal has to be taken in good spirit. Slate quarries, coal mines and open pit iron and copper mines are examples of working areas not open to individual collectors.

There is an advantage in joining a mineral club. These clubs flourish—especially in areas famed for mining activity—and the collector should have no difficulty in locating one. There are also a number in Great Britain and Australia. Sometimes club parties are allowed to visit quarries or mines not otherwise accessible, usually at the weekend or on some non-working day, when under experienced supervision members are able to hunt for specimens. This is a pleasant way of collecting, as one is among other enthusiasts and interest and excitement run high on these expeditions. Serious collectors and students of geology will find it worth while to apply for membership in a professional association of geologists. This will keep one up to date on advances in the field.

Old mine dumps are a rich source of specimens, of course, and in areas where there are many abandoned workings, there is ample opportunity for hunting. (But here again strict attention should be paid to 'keep out' notices, which often indicate dangerous shafts or subsidences in the neighborhood and not merely a cantankerous landowner.) It is useless to spend time on thickly overgrown mine dumps; not only is it almost impossible to see any specimens but the material on the surface will in any case probably be too badly weathered to be of value. The best dumps are those that have been excavated for hardcore or filling material for one purpose or another.

Cliffs and caves are worthy of close inspection, especially in mining areas. Specimens will probably be difficult to extract from cliff faces or the walls of caves, but a careful search at the foot of likely cliffs or on cave floors is often most rewarding. Poking among the debris of rock falls is another idea. Occasionally natural rock slides occur which reveal beautiful specimens but man induced upheavals are even more common. Seek out your nearest highway under construction and pick over the debris on the weekend when they aren't blasting. Watch out for faulty explosives and give them a wide berth.

If you collect fossils you are indulging in an interest which was cultivated as far back as the times of the ancient Greeks and Romans, who preserved and recorded some of their finds. Nowadays palaeontology is a highly developed science, but there is no reason at all why the keen amateur should not dabble in it and derive a great deal of pleasure from it. It really does open the book of time; you can actually see and hold forms which existed on the earth millions of years ago. It is from these impressions preserved in stone that experts have built up those pictures of prehistoric times, dinosaurs, lizards, sponges, corals, and all.

As with minerals, fossils may be obtained from places where land is being excavated, or where it is being eroded. Some types of rock are abundant in fossils whilst others are completely bare of them, so do some research beforehand. Quarries, gravel pits and road excavations are among the meccas for the fossil collector and the same rules on permission to enter apply as those suggested for the mineral hunter. The Coal Measures are rich in fossils but little will be found by examining every lump of coal before putting it on the fire! The fossils are mainly found in the stone which underlies the coal itself and so it is the coal-mine waste that is likely to be productive or along the ugly scars left by strip mining. For those living in areas of sedimentary rock fossils are more varied than the minerals and soon will become the field of dominant interest.

When fossils have to be hammered out of rocks it is not sheer brute strength that is needed but some skill in wielding a hammer and chisel, and this is a skill not acquired in a few minutes. It will soon be found that carefully placed blows with a corner of the square end of the hammer will be necessary on some rocks, whilst for others the chisel edge will prove most suitable. The usual procedure is to split the rock along the bedding planes to reveal the fossils, and the cold chisel will be a tremendous help here, so long as it is placed carefully and not haphazardly. Just as different types of rock contain different types of fossils, so different types of rock split differently and you should get used to the handling of these before actually getting to work on a fossil.

Some fossils are, in fact, so fragile that it is impossible to remove them from their rocky matrix until they have been hardened.

Specimens of various minerals

Books on paleontology will give the details of the hardening process. (A word of warning to smokers—the solutions used are highly inflammable and 'cigarettes out' must be the rule when hardening fossils.)

The sieving of sand is an excellent way of discovering minute fossils which would otherwise not show up, on a beach for instance; but shake the sieve very lightly, as fossils are fragile things. Always pay special attention to nodules found on the beach or elsewhere. They frequently contain fossils and a firm tap with the hammer will usually split them open. Many will be barren but all the effort is well worthwhile when one finally reveals a well-preserved piece of carbonised wood, or something even more exciting such as fish remains.

The collector of minerals or fossils is advised to arm himself with a reliable textbook to assist in identification. There are excellent little paperback pocket volumes dealing with both subjects, and details of these and other books on the same subjects are given at the back of this book.

SEEDLINGS

The person who is interested in collecting seedlings to grow into miniature trees has a wide field of operations. Keen growers and collectors of bonsai or dwarf trees usually like to dig their specimens in bleak, stony mountainous areas where the seedling is naturally stunted by climatic conditions such as above the tree line in the Rockies, or windswept exposed places along the coast. Other up-land areas are likely to provide these fascinating midget speci-mens, as are similar locations in other countries. Old and neglected yards also often provide suitable specimens. Quite a few nurseries are now cultivating bonsai so it is possible to buy well-established specimens to start a collection if one is more interested in the actual cultivation than in the collecting of the seedlings. Prices for nursery specimens are usually from about $7·50, and the older the dwarf tree the more expensive it is. Really ancient specimens which are still thriving long after their original owner has gone are sometimes sold for several hundred dollars. (Again it must be emphasised that when collecting seedlings in the wild permission should always be obtained before digging on private property of any sort. Some public parks have rules protecting plant life so one hould check at every park before starting to collect specimens.

THE REST

Locations for sheep's wool, feathers and spiders' webs need no explanation. Hardly a place exists that will not add some item to your collection. Different breeds of sheep have different wool distinctive in color and texture. Feathers can best be found at the nesting and feeding places of birds.

Spiders' webs come in great variety. Look out for the distinctive triangular web of *Hyptiotes paradoxus*, built usually on the twigs of yew and other conifers. The beautiful gossamer webs, or orb snares, that the large garden spider and the smaller *Meta segmentata* build between plants in gardens or hedgerow, are the ones to collect for decorative purposes (see p 71). Embellishments peculiar to each species are added to these webs, rather like signatures. The best webs are spun by young spiders; when they get old their webs become smaller, with fewer radii and spirals, and are often untidy and defective. Avoid these when collecting webs and go only for perfect specimens.

CHAPTER FOUR

Plant Collections:
How to Keep and Display Them

CHOOSING A SYSTEM

The new collector is content at first simply to keep items together—perhaps in a cardboard box, between the pages of a book, or maybe stuck into a notebook. But there comes a time, when the collection begins to outgrow the original method of storage and you inevitably look around for alternative—and better—ways of keeping such treasures, and perhaps also for ways of arranging them so that they may be admired and enjoyed by others.

The type of storage and display you go in for is necessarily determined by the amount of space you can spare for your collection, the amount of money you can afford to spend on storage units and the amount of time you are prepared to put into the business of keeping the display in order. That splendid large glass-topped case in the museum will never look right in a small apartment, but if you live in a big house or have an outside room of some kind, then you can cast your eye on grander types of display. The suggestions in this chapter should be adapted to your own requirements. You will also need to know the best

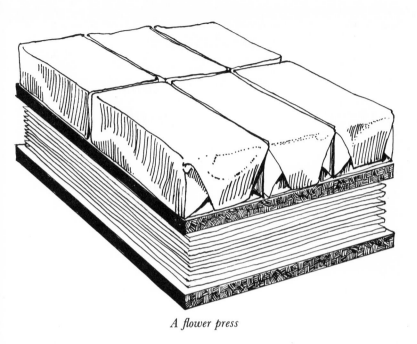

A flower press

ways of preparing your plant specimens in order to preserve them and keep them looking their best.

PRESSING FLOWERS, GRASSES AND FERNS

Once you get your specimens home it is advisable to dry and press them without delay. They are easier to prepare for pressing when they are fresh and crisp—and this is especially true of flowers; if left overnight they wilt and the petals and leaves tend to curl.

Pressing flowers between the pages of a book is an old schooldays habit which should be forgotten when you start a proper collection. Not only does it mark the pages of the book and stain the binding, but it does not do the job properly and the flowers emerge creased and unnatural-looking, which is both disappointing and annoying.

Ideally, botanical paper, made especially for the purpose of pressing flowers and plants, is the material to get, but white blotting paper can be used with complete success. Buy as large a sheet as possible and fold it so that you can cut it into sheets of approximately 16-18in × 10-12in. Sheets of this size should be large enough for most of the specimens you have to prepare; if you envisage having larger items then keep some complete sheets of blotting paper ready as well. Newspaper can be substituted in emergency, but it is less absorbent and sometimes the print comes off on the specimen. Two pieces of heavy board are necessary for sandwiching the blotting paper firmly; plywood or masonite are not really recommended. Some place should be set aside on which to stand the press, for once filled with specimens it must be left until they are dry and ready for mounting.

Weights are necessary for the top of the sandwich. Stones are not suitable for this as their weight will not be distributed evenly. Books are not always heavy enough. If you are the fortunate owner of any old flat irons these would be admirable, but the best thing to use is three or four bricks. They should be well brushed and scrubbed before use, but even then they tend to leave a residue of brickdust, which could be harmful if it seeped between the covers of the press and on to the specimens, so I suggest that you wrap your bricks neatly in heavy brown paper, sealing the ends tightly with scotch tape or, alternatively, wrap them in strong cotton or similar material and closely sew up the ends and overlap.

With the press ready, the next step is to prepare the specimens. Put two pieces of blotting paper on the bottom board and then, on a *third* sheet, start arranging your specimens. This is where skill and artistry come in; time and care taken over this operation are very well spent. Once a specimen is dry it is impossible to alter it. If you are including the roots of a plant these should be cleaned before pressing; it may even be necessary to wash them in order to remove all the earth, and if this has to be done be sure that the roots are as dry as possible before putting the plant in the press. Pat them dry on an old cloth or towel and use blotting paper to absorb any moisture remaining after the patting process. Be careful to see also that leaves and petals, especially fleshy ones, are free of surplus moisture.

Collectors use varying methods of handling specimens when arranging them in the press, but I have found from experience that by far the best tool for this purpose is an artist's camel-hair paint brush with a good point. Place the specimen on the sheet of blotting paper and with the paint brush arrange it as naturally as possible. Spread out the leaves and flowers and also the roots if you are doing a complete plant; gently stroke out the petals so that they lie quite flat on the blotting paper, ensure that leaves are not curled at the edges and that stems follow their natural curve. It is false economy to try and press too many specimens on one sheet of blotting paper. If the paper is asked to absorb too much the specimens will not press satisfactorily. So leave plenty of space between specimens, especially if they are fleshy items which will exude quite a lot of moisture.

When the flowers, leaves, ferns or whatever you are pressing are arranged attractively on the blotting paper take several more sheets of clean blotting paper and cover the specimens *very carefully*. Use at least three sheets; four would be even better. This is a most important stage in the whole operation, because if the specimens are creased or curled or in any way disarranged when you cover them they will be spoilt. So place the sheets over the specimens very gently and take great care not to move them in any way once they are in position. On the top sheet of blotting paper you can then arrange another group of specimens and cover them in the same way. You can go on doing this until quite a thick pad of specimens has been built. Then place the board on top, and on top of that the bricks or other weights, and leave the press for at least three days. At the end of that time the plants will be getting dry and should be put between fresh sheets of blotting paper. They will still probably be floppy and should be moved and re-covered with utmost care. Leave the press for another three days and at the end of that period your specimens will be ready for mounting. This timetable applies to most plants, though some of the fleshy varieties may need a little longer. Never attempt to mount a specimen until it is completely pressed and dry. Remember, too, that the blotting paper will not last for ever and will need renewing after it has been used about six times. Botanical drying paper lasts a little longer, so could work out cheaper in the long run.

DRYING IN SAND OR BORAX

Some flowers are too large or too bulky to press but there is another method of preserving plants which is worth attention. This is drying in sand or borax, and it works extremely well for roses, for all members of the daisy family, and for such sturdy wild plants as common mullein. You will need a strong box in wood, stout cardboard or tin, with a slip-on lid that fits snugly. Personally I prefer to use borax for this method of preservation, but it is rather expensive if you are doing a lot of large flowers (even though it can be used over and over again) because you will need so much; and I have seen excellent results achieved in ordinary sand. Some experts advise the use of builders' 'silver sand', but others advocate ordinary fine beach sand; either will work.

If you are going to try the borax method start off with some small flower such as a rosebud and buy from any pharmacy half a pound of powdered borax. Lay a fairly thick carpet of this on the bottom of your drying box—a depth of about half an inch should be all right. On this place the flower or plant to be preserved. If it has thin and fragile leaves or petals arrange these naturally with the aid of your paint brush. When the specimen is arranged to your satisfaction start sprinkling over it—very lightly—the rest of the

42

powdered borax, until it is buried to a depth of about one inch. Do not make any attempt to smooth the powder or to disturb it in any way. Put the lid on the drying box, and it should be tight fitting enough not to need any string or rubber bands to keep it in place. Very gently put the box in a place where it will not have to be moved and leave it unopened for at least three weeks. At the end of that time open the box, very carefully remove the specimen with the paint brush, gently shaking off any powder which adheres to it. It should then be quite dry and papery, and many species thus preserved retain their natural colours to a remarkable degree.

If sand is used it must first be washed and thoroughly dried. Follow the same method of 'carpeting' the bottom of the box and placing the specimen. Then *heat* the sand which is to cover the flower or plant. This can be done in the oven and it should be quite hot when it is sprinkled over the specimen. Again put aside the box or tin and leave it for at least ten days or a fortnight before opening it up to remove the specimen. Autumn leaves especially retain their colours well by the sand method and it is also good for big leaves of leathery texture, such as some of the magnolia family.

MOUNTING

The mounting of specimens can be to individual taste. Professionally they are usually attached, by means of gummed paper or fine canvas strips, to sheets of thick white paper and kept in folders. If you decide to keep your specimens in an album it is well worth getting one with good quality paper. After all, the specimens take a lot of time and trouble to prepare and are worthy of a nice setting. Never use thin paper and above all never just put them in a notebook.

Another professional way of mounting dried plants is on cards, one specimen per card, and this is the method I prefer. For this, buy a sheet of white cardboard at a stationer's shop and cut it to the size or sizes required. If possible keep all cards of uniform size.

Some collectors like to use coloured cards, choosing a colour to contrast with specimens being mounted; personally, I prefer white card for all coloured specimens and pale grey for white flowers.

Avoid handling the dried specimens more than is absolutely necessary and try and slide them on to their respective cards rather than lifting them up. They can be fixed to the card or paper with just the tiniest spot of colorless glue (eg Elmer's glue), or they can be fastened with tiny strips of transparent adhesive tape (eg Scotch tape) or with gummed canvas strips (sold especially for the purpose by botanical suppliers) placed across each stalk just below the flower and at the end of the stem. For ferns, a dab of glue at the top and a piece of tape or canvas across the stem will hold the specimen firmly. If possible, keep your dried plants, whether on cards or in an album, in an airtight box or other receptacle, otherwise they may grow mould or be eaten away by minute insects. A few crystals of silica gel (obtainable from a druggist) put in the box with the specimens will help to absorb moisture and so preserve them from damp. In scientific herbariums paradichlorbenzene is used for this purpose.

Each specimen must of course be named. It is usual to give both the English (or popular) and Latin names and to add details of where the specimen was found (name of place and actual location —'on cliffs', 'in a wood', etc) and also the date on which it was found—day, month and year being necessary here. These entries can be made on the card or album page, or on a small adhesive label for fixing. Remember that the scientific value of a collection can only be measured by its documentation. If you are using an album be sure to have cellophane interleaved between each sheet, so that the plants do not rub. Cellophane is also ideal for covering each card if you choose to mount your specimens that way; it should overlap the card and be stuck down at the back with scotch tape or something similar. But avoid shuffling the cards about. Even if they are covered with cellophane the specimens will tend to rub in time if they are roughly handled.

Dried and mounted plant

PRESERVING FOR ARRANGEMENTS

There are other methods of preserving flowers and leaves and these are used mainly for material for flower arrangements, though the specimens can equally well be displayed in a collection. The three methods suggested are drying by hanging, skeletonising and glycerining.

Drying by hanging is the easiest of all methods of preserving plants, and it works very well with some garden and wild flowers, as well as with grasses. Gather flowers for hanging when buds have just opened, never when they are full blown or on the point of fading. Some garden flowers, such as delphiniums and golden rod, hold their colour after being dried and look most effective. Some wild plants also keep their colour; experiment will show you which can be most successfully hung. Be sure the flowers are free from moisture, as damp will rot them; then tie them together in small bunches and hang them head downwards in a dark place: they should be fully dry in a few weeks. Some plants, including grasses of all types, can be dried by standing in jugs or vases. Grasses are best dried naturally by laying them out in the sun, but it is not always possible to do that. Seed pods will dry well if hung up in a dark and dry place.

It is often possible to find skeleton leaves in the woods or in hedges but frequently these naturally skeletonised specimens are torn or otherwise disfigured. You will probably make a better job of it yourself. Not all leaves are suitable for the purpose but tough well-ribbed ones such as magnolia, laurel and holly give very good results. The method is to boil the leaves in strong soda water. An old saucepan should be used for this operation—it will not be fit for any other purpose afterwards. Boil the leaves until the flesh can be gently scraped off with a fingernail. When they have reached that stage remove them from the water, lay them on a thick wad of newspaper and very gently start scraping off all the green flesh with a knife. Try hard not to tear the leaf

46

but do not expect 100 per cent success, even when you have become quite skilled. When all the flesh is off wash the skeleton leaf in clean water (holding it under a gently running tap is the best way) and then dry it between sheets of clean blotting paper. The whole process is a little messy and rather unpleasantly smelly when the leaves are boiling, but some very delightful results *can* be achieved with plenty of practice.

The preserving of leaves in a glycerine solution is done by most flower arrangers, and leaves so treated will last for several years if prepared properly and stored carefully. Beech, laurel, eucalyptus, magnolia, oak, are all satisfactory subjects, and you will discover many others by the process of trial and error. The solution is made up of one part of glycerine to three parts of warm water. Small branches are usually selected for this process, but it is possible to do individual leaves if so desired. Make a small slit with a knife in the bottom of the stem or branch so that the preserving liquid will be absorbed easily, and then place the specimens in a jar with about two inches of the solution. Allow them to stand undisturbed until it is seen that the mixture is being absorbed and the leaves are gradually turning brown (this usually occurs after a few days in the solution). From then on the leaves should be watched carefully because if they absorb too much solution they will 'sweat' and soon go mouldy. When they have turned brown they are ready for removal. For beech branches the period of absorption is usually two to three weeks (individual leaves do not take nearly so long). The leaves should feel smooth and glossy to the touch but *not* sticky. If they do feel sticky they have been left too long in the solution and will soon deteriorate when removed from it. On the other hand, if they have not absorbed enough of the glycerine solution they will soon shrivel. Remove the branches or leaves from the jar and dry the ends of the stems thoroughly before storing in a dry place.

PRESERVING FUNGI, LICHEN AND MOSSES

The person who is interested in fungi may hesitate to gather specimens of the fleshier type, believing, mistakenly, that it is almost impossible to preserve them. But actually there are several courses of action open to the fungi enthusiast. The easiest way is by drying. The experts suggest a temperature of 104°F as being ideal for the process but it is not always easy accurately to assess temperature when drying specimens at home; the main requirement is a good circulation of air so that the moisture is removed. This process may be carried out in a can on a low gas or electric stove, or even in front of a fire. The fungi do, of course, lose color and also become rather shrivelled by this method. If you want natural-looking specimens try preserving them in liquid in airtight bottles or jars. Formalin or formaldehyde are the preservatives used by amateurs. Both may be obtained from drugstores and the 5 per cent solution of formaldehyde which is recommended for the treatment of most specimens can be obtained already made-up. Some fungi may require stronger or weaker solutions, but again you will find this out by trial and error. Remember if you use formaldehyde as a preservative that it is an irritant and must not get on to the hands; use thick gloves. The vapour must not be inhaled either, and of course the solution should never be allowed to get near eyes or mouth.

Bottled specimens should be labelled with details (name, where found, when found, etc), and dried specimens can be stored in small boxes or polythene bags with a few grains of napthalene.

A popular method of making a fungi collection is to keep spore prints. This again applies to toadstool-type specimens and the way to do it is to lay the *cap only* of the fungus, gills downward, on a sheet of good quality white paper. The cap should be left undisturbed for about twenty-four hours. Lift it up very gently and it will be found to have deposited a powder on the paper, forming a perfect imprint. This should be sprayed with clear varnish and when the varnish is completely dry the cards can be labelled and stored. Anyone who is a keen photographer may like to 'collect' fungi by taking photographs of specimens in their natural habitat, another idea which is gaining in popularity among naturalists. This method also applies to other collections (see below).

Some lichens and fern-like mosses can be pressed in the same way as flowers. Specimens not suitable for pressing should be kept in small boxes (such as matchboxes) and allowed to dry naturally. When boxed specimens are dry they should be stored in small plastic bags with a few grains of napthalene to prevent mould from forming.

PHOTOGRAPHIC COLLECTING

For those who don't like to disturb nature, photographic collecting can replace pressing, drying, formaldehyding and the like. Use a camera which will get reasonably close to the subject and take color pictures of your specimen. For scientific records carry a ruler to photograph next to your subject and a notebook in which to record details such as photo number, specimen name and where it was found. For the ultimate record a small blackboard containing both the ruler and the information can be included in the photograph. Photographs can be arranged in an album according to species, genus, or whatever and contain both identifying pictures and more arty shots.

CONES AND SEED PODS

Cones, which should be collected, as you remember, when they are young and before they have opened, are cleaned by brushing with an old toothbrush or soft wire brush to ensure that no insects are hiding between the scales. If they have been picked up from the ground they should be wiped with a damp cloth to remove any mud or earth and then dried naturally in the open air. As soon as possible after collection they should be brushed or sprayed with clear varnish, making sure that coverage is complete. This prevents them from opening and preserves them from insect attack—though I have seen some specimens treated in this way which have been attacked when insects have found a spot bare of varnish.

Seed pods can be similarly treated but some will eventually shrivel. You will quickly find which kinds will keep almost indefinately and which soon deteriorate. Specimens can be displayed in small boxes, or in bags.

CHAPTER FIVE

Geological Collections:
How to Keep and Display Them

IDENTIFICATION OF ROCKS AND MINERALS

First of all you will want to identify precisely the specimens which you have brought in from your expeditions. This will not always be easy. Such well-known things as granite and sandstone you will be able to classify (in general terms) immediately; but with minerals especially you will come up against snags. Never be put off or feel that the whole subject is too complicated for you to master; as with everything, knowledge comes with experience.

Minerals are chemical elements or compounds found naturally in the earth's crust. Some are a series of related compounds in which one metallic element may wholly or partially replace another. This leads to great variation in colour and texture, but there are simple tests which help identify many of the commoner minerals. The beginner often labours under the illusion that all minerals are in the form of large crystals and that nothing else is worthy of a second glance. This is not so at all; some minerals take the form of a thin coating, almost like a powder; some may be in the form of minute scales, and crystals may be too small for the naked eye to perceive.

It is most important to possess a good magnifying glass and if you

51

are fortunate enough to own or have access to a microscope then so much the better. The experts employ many other forms of equipment, much of it expensive, some of it complicated; but for the amateur too much equipment is only confusing, especially at first. When one becomes an advanced amateur, then is the time to consider scientific equipment.

First examine your specimens carefully under the glass or microscope and decide on the shapes of the crystals. Then try to identify these crystal shapes with the help of books. The next step is to determine hardness. It is helpful to learn by heart what is known as Mohs' scale of hardness; this is a standard scale which was worked out at the beginning of last century by a German mineralogist called Friedrich Mohs and it is now fairly generally accepted. The scale is as follows: (1) talc (2) gypsum (3) calcite (4) fluorite (5) apatite (6) orthoclase (7) quartz (8) topaz (9) corundum (10) diamond. This scale represents only the degrees of hardness between one mineral and another, the hardest coming last: for instance, 2 (gypsum) is harder than 1 (talc), and 4 (fluorite) is harder than 3 (calcite) and less hard than 5 (apatite). So, if any one of your specimens will scratch all the minerals in the scale up to 4 and is *itself* scratched by apatite then its hardness is between 4 and 5.

But if you do not even know if the mineral in front of you is one of those in the scale, here is a simpler way of determining hardness. Your fingernail is rated approximately at hardness $2\frac{1}{2}$, so if you can scratch (and be careful to see that there is a distinct scratch on the specimen) a mineral with your fingernail then that mineral is in 1-2 group; a copper coin (eg penny) is rated as hardness 4 and will scratch minerals in groups 1, 2 and 3; the blade of an average penknife is rated at hardness $5\frac{1}{2}$ and will therefore scratch specimens from all groups below 6. A steel file is rated at hardness $6\frac{1}{2}$ and will scratch minerals up to group 7. Diamond, of course, is the hardest of all minerals and will scratch every other. In Mohs' scale, 10 is the hardest of all, 9 and 8 we can think of as very hard,

52

7 and 6 are hard, 5 and 4 medium-hard, 3 and 2 soft, and 1 very soft.

Having tested for hardness the next step is to test for streak. This is the colour left by the mineral when it is scratched across a piece of hard, rough, white material such as an unglazed tile, or even the back of an ordinary grate tile. Streak plates may be bought in boxes of varying quantities, but the tile will serve the same purpose. The streak made by a mineral may be quite different from the colour of the mineral as one sees it—that is, the colour of its surface. You will again need to use a reference book to see what the colour streaks of different minerals are.

Weight also helps in identification, although specific gravity can really only be accurately determined by the expert. However, some minerals are obviously much heavier than others when weighed in the hand and this will again help identification. For instance, metallic minerals such as iron (haematite) and lead (galena) will be found to weigh much heavier in the hand than specimens of other minerals in similar-sized pieces.

The lustre or texture of the surface of a mineral sample is important. This can be classified roughly as glassy, metallic, dull, etc, and such descriptions speak for themselves. Some minerals, such as chalcedony, may have a waxy appearance, or feel slightly soapy to the touch. Many minerals can be identified according to the way in which they split when broken. This is known as cleavage; some minerals split in the form of blocks, some in the form of rhombohedrons, and so on. You need a little practice, however, before you are able to establish with certainty what are the cleavage planes.

PREPARATION OF MINERAL SPECIMENS

Now we come to the preparation of the specimens before they are stored or put on display, and here I must add a note of warning. Many collectors (and books) advocate the washing of all specimens in water as soon as they are turned out of the collecting bag.

It is certainly important that all specimens should be cleaned, but a scrub-up in water is not *always* the answer. Water may even have a destructive effect on some minerals and hasten their decomposition. It is recommended that specimens be washed only in the following solution: 100ml industrial alcohol, 10g soft soap, 1ml ammonia. It is advisable to wear rubber gloves when using this solution and these can now be bought in a fine quality that allows for sensitivity of touch even with delicate specimens. Only the very toughest of rocks should be scrubbed. For most mineral specimens a very soft old toothbrush or a small baby brush, wielded very gently, is all that is necessary. Brownish fungoid stains caused by dampness may be removed with the use of a 20vol solution of hydrogen peroxide with a small drop of ammonia, and when stains have been removed or at least have considerably faded (some will prove to be of too long standing to disappear altogether) the specimen should be gently rinsed in industrial alcohol.

Some amateur collectors have trouble with minerals 'weeping', and this not only makes a nasty mess in the cabinet or storage box but is also the beginning of the end of the specimen, for it will eventually decompose altogether if the flow of moisture is not stopped. Spraying with clear varnish is the easiest form of protection for the amateur to use. Not all minerals have this vexing habit, but all sulphides (iron pyrites, copper pyrites, galena, bornite, arsenopyrite, sphalerite etc) and halides (secondary copper minerals) are prone to decomposition and should be treated if one wishes to preserve them in a collection.

Every specimen should be clearly labelled with its name, where found and date found. There are two ways of doing this: either you can write it very small on a tiny adhesive label and attach it to the actual specimen, or you can put a small circle of white paint on each sample and print the details on that, in Indian ink. The second method means that essential details are never lost, but I personally prefer the adhesive label. Alternatively you can number each specimen and enter descriptive details in a card index or catalogue; much valuable information can be added against the entry for each specimen and the sample itself is not defaced with conspicuous labels. Numbering is usually done on a tiny dab of quick-drying white enamel paint, but do keep this as small as possible.

STORAGE AND DISPLAY OF MINERALS

The actual storing of the specimens depends on the fancy and the pocket of the individual collector. Proper specimen cases with glass-covered display tops and close-fitting drawers beneath, are, of course, very costly unless one is good at carpentry and can make one's own. They do take up a tremendous amount of room and are often not practicable in a modern home anyway. A better storage cabinet for the amateur collector is a glass-fronted book-case with three or more shelves. Old-fashioned glass-fronted cupboards can often be bought quite reasonably at auctions, and so long as the glass is clear and uncracked a coat of paint will soon brighten up shabby woodwork. It is a good idea to paint some shelves white and some black, to show off specimens to best advantage. Kaolin, for instance, would not look very good on a white-painted shelf, but on a black one it 'comes to life'. You may prefer to cover the shelves by sticking velvet along them and this is advisable if the shelves are pitted, scored or uneven. Never use patterned paper or any type of patterned covering.

If you do not want to have the collection on show then a series of small boxes of uniform size, shape and colour can be used (see also p 62). It is not advisable to leave specimens out on a shelf, uncovered. Dust soon becomes a problem, and they are not improved by constant handling or dusting. In fact this sort of treatment would probably ruin crystal specimens or those with a coating of small scales. If kept in boxes the samples should rest on cotton-wool and should always be kept the right way up and treated carefully.

Collectors' specimens should be, as far as possible, of uniform size, and when breaking from a large mass it is usual to aim at a piece about the size of a hen's egg. Collectors are turning more to the keeping of microscopic samples on glass slides, this being a more convenient way of storing a large collection, but to me nothing is so satisfying as the actual sample as it was found and in a piece large enough to be of aesthetic value to collector and non-collector alike.

Classification of a collection is again a matter of personal choice. It can be classified, if desired, under such headings as metallic minerals, non-metallic minerals, rock-forming minerals, gem minerals; but most people like to start with a general collection and do not commence classifying until they have become more advanced in their knowledge and have a good number of exhibits.

PREPARATION AND DISPLAY OF FOSSILS

Having got your specimens home you will have a bit of work to do on them, but it will be most rewarding. First of all examine them carefully as you unwrap them. Any that are pyritized must receive attention at once because they soon start to decompose on exposure to the air.

The old-fashioned method of preserving pyritized fossils is to dip the specimen in hot (but *not* boiling) candle wax. Be quite sure that it is completely coated, and drain off excess wax. More up-to-date is the painting or spraying of the specimen with clear polyurethane varnish, obtainable in small cans at about 75 cents from hardware stores or home-decorating stores. Whichever method of preservation you choose for pyritized fossils you should examine them regularly and check for any sign of decomposition. You can give them first-aid treatment by painting over with colourless nail varnish, but they should be dealt with properly at the first possible opportunity.

If you have excavated fossils, as opposed to picking them up on a beach, they are likely to have some of the rock in which they were bedded (matrix) surrounding them and in most cases they should be removed from this—although if you have several specimens of the same kind you might want to keep one intact in matrix, for display purposes. When the matrix is hard you will have to remove it by means of a small sharp knife, a stiletto, or even a stout needle, depending on the size and nature of the fossil. Press the chosen tool carefully down on to the matrix at right angles to the fossil: if this is done properly, pieces should break off neatly without damaging the fossil itself. A small drill obtained from a hardware or do-it-yourself shop would, however, be easier on the hands.

If you have the misfortune to break a specimen or if you pick up an already broken one you can make a good job of mending it by using one of the modern two-component adhesives. Epoxy is specially recommended, as it is clean and easy to work with and is outstandingly effective as a bonding agent. At more than a dollar for small tubes it may seem a little expensive, but it is well worth the extra outlay and one pack will repair very many fossils.

Casts can be made from fossil moulds and displayed alongside them in a collection. Plaster of Paris can be used for this but it is not always entirely satisfactory; paraffin wax is another not wholly ideal substance. Museums favour the type of wax used by dentists for taking impressions of gums and this is obtainable from dental manufacturing companies. Putty, modelling clay and modelling wax are other media you can try. Dental plaster, bought from druggists, is very suitable. Always remember to dust the mould with French chalk before taking a cast, otherwise the cast material adheres to the mould and does not come out cleanly.

Those accustomed to handling tools may like to cut and polish some of the larger ammonites in order to reveal the interior structure. Well finished specimens are most attractive. This comes

Fossils

into the field of lapidary work and a diamond saw is necessary to get good results. The operation is a highly skilled one and it is not advisable to invest in cutting and polishing equipment until you are sure you can use it properly and will have enough specimens to prepare. On the other hand, for those capable of using it such equipment can open a whole new field of interest in the collection of fossils.

Another type of fossil, the silicified or phosphatized specimen which is sometimes found in limestone, requires special treatment in preparation for the cabinet. The matrix surrounding such a specimen can be dissolved away with diluted acetic acid, but great care must be taken in handling the acid and it must not be brought into direct contact with the fossil itself, otherwise it may dissolve the fossil and not the matrix!

The suggestions given for the display of minerals also apply to fossils. Whether on display, or stored and brought out only for inspection purposes, each fossil specimen should be clearly labelled and catalogued. Suppliers of naturalists' equipment sell cardboard trays in varying sizes, some of them 'stackable', and these are, of course, the ideal way of storing fossil and small mineral specimens, each item in its own compartment, and with a ticket giving name and details. For very small fossils you can stick matchboxes together and build up your own miniature chest of drawers, covering it with paper or self-adhesive plastic material to make it neat. Line each tray with cotton-wool to keep fragile fossils safe. Read books on the subject and examine museum displays to find out how to classify your specimens in their correct periods.

A PEBBLE COLLECTION

Many pebbles when picked up do not reveal their true beauty because in the course of their weathering by the action of river or sea and their continual grinding against other stones they have acquired a covering film or 'skin' which has to be removed before the specimens are ready for display. Sometimes this film so alters the colour of a pebble as to make its true nature almost unrecognisable. A knife with a strong blade should be used to scrape it off. It will take time and a good deal of patience but is well worth the effort. If the pebble proves to be of a soft type of stone try to avoid scratching the surface too much (and, needless to say, contrive to hold the pebble in such a manner that a slip of the knife will not cut your hand).

When all, or as much as possible, of the film has been removed,

wash the pebble in clean water to which a little household detergent has been added. As an alternative to this laborious task of
scraping you can try and collect two of each variety, keeping one
'as found', with film and all, and display the other cracked open
to reveal a freshly fractured surface and the true appearance of the
rock of which the pebble is composed.

The arrangement of your pebble collection depends on how
scientific you want to be. Some people like to make a general
collection, including all and every type of pebble they come across
and trying to get specimens from as many different locations as
possible. Others like to classify their pebbles by the types of rock
to which they belong: igneous, sedimentary, and so on. Once
started on this method you can break the collection down into
many sub-divisions. It is the method favoured by most museums
and has much to commend it. Some people like to specialise
in pebbles from one particular area of country or section of
coastline (perhaps near where they live) or even from one beach.
Although the scope is more limited in this type of classification,
there is a challenge in trying to make a collection as completely
representative as possible of one particular area. Some people go
in for semi-precious stones only, but unless your locality provides
them this limits your collecting activities to vacation periods.

Storage methods are the same as for minerals and fossils and
each specimen must be clearly labelled, or numbered and in-
dexed.

There is a growing fashion now for polishing pebbles. Personally
I am not fond of this; an artificially polished pebble does not have
for me as much fascination as a pebble in its natural state. However, if you like to treat your specimens in this way, a simple and
effective method is to paint them with a thin coat of clear varnish.
This is, of course, only suitable for pebbles which are to repose in a
display: methods of polishing for use as jewellery or ornaments
are described briefly in a later chapter.

Coloured sands

FROM PEBBLES TO SAND

Sand collecting is a fascinating and unusual hobby, and quite without problems. Because it does not deteriorate, sand is easy to store and no special preparation is necessary. Keep it in glass tubes or small glass bottles; display them on a set of narrow shelves or store them in wooden boxes—cigar boxes are ideal.

You can buy glass Clinitest test tubes at a drugstore which cost $1·20 for six. If this is too expensive you can use regular plastic

61

pill containers, also obtained from your druggist. They should be as far as possible of uniform size and this is, of course, the advantage of using test tubes. It is usual to collect two to three ounces of each type of sand, but obviously the amount will be governed by the containers you are going to use.

The best way of keeping records is to number each tube or bottle and then enter the numbers in catalogue form in a notebook or index system, recording where the specimen was found, whether it was above or below the tideline, the time of year and any relevant details about nearby cliffs or the geology of the surrounding countryside. Some people like to classify their sands geologically but I like to display them so that the many varied colours show to advantage, placing for instance a tube of pure white sand beside a tube of black, and a tube of bright yellow beside a tube of red, and so on. There are absolutely no rules for sand collectors, and you can please yourself entirely.

I saw an unusual method of displaying a collection of sand, designed by a collector. He had drawn large outline maps of each state and on them had printed in Indian ink the names of the places from which he had a sample of sand. He had then brushed a one-inch square of gum above each name and on it sprinkled some of the sand collected there. Several of the maps were completely covered with sand samples and these were mounted on masonite, protected with transparent plastic about one-tenth of an inch thick (less fragile than glass and screw holes can be bored in it) and hung on the walls of his study. This is an ideal way of displaying small samples, especially for collectors who cannot travel about armed with scoop and plastic bags but yet may often have an opportunity of taking up just a small quantity of sand and popping it in the corner of an envelope.

CHAPTER SIX

Flotsam and Jetsam

DRIFTWOOD AND WOOD SAMPLES

Driftwood cleaning and preparation is covered on pp 102-3. A wash and scrub are all that is necessary to remove sand particles and generally freshen. One does not normally display driftwood as a collection, but suitable pieces are used for flower arranging, or as ornaments in home or garden, or are sculptured, as explained also on pp 102-3.

Wood samples are usually only thin slivers, so no cleaning is necessary. They should not be mounted until completely dry, and then a dab of adhesive on the back will secure them to cards, or they can all be stuck on one large piece of stiff cardboard or painted masonite. Labels can be stuck beneath each specimen giving name, where found, when, type of country (garden, woods, common etc), or if separate cards are kept each one can be numbered and the details entered in a notebook. Samples should not ideally be varnished or polished, though if one really does want them looking glossy a colourless varnish of good quality, bought at a shop which sells artists' materials, should be applied.

THE CHALLENGE OF ALGAE

The study of seaweeds really started seriously about a hundred years ago and the subject bears a little-heard name—algology.

For a long time the collecting and preserving of specimens was confined to museums and other scientific organisations. Now, however, plenty of other people are interested, and as collectors often express disappointment that specimens do not preserve well or that some cannot even be preserved at all, here are some methods by which you can keep a collection of seaweeds as a permanent pleasure.

It is important to remember that many seaweeds wilt or decay if left long in the sun, even if they are still in sea water. Pieces you collect, after being cleaned up on site, should be shaded as much as possible, carried home in the way suggested in Chapter 1, and dealt with at the first opportunity.

The most popular form of mounting for the amateur is on paper, although some like to keep delicate specimens on pieces of thin glass or clear plastic, floating them on and allowing them to dry naturally as they have adhered to the glass. In museums specimens are dried in this way on microscope slides. For paper mounting, good quality unglazed paper should be used. You will also need a supply of blotting paper, some cheesecloth or similar material and a shallow dish slightly larger than the biggest sheet of mounting paper you are going to use. The dish should be filled with sea water, *not* fresh water; many of the more delicate seaweeds change or lose their colour in fresh water. If you have not any sea water to hand do not try to produce salt water by adding ordinary table or cooking salt to fresh water. This just does not have the desired effect. To 'manufacture' salt water acceptable to seaweeds you must obtain from a health store a small quantity of 'sea salt' and dissolve one and a half ounces of this in every quart of fresh water.

Cut the mounting paper slightly larger than the specimen to be mounted and submerge it in the dish of salt water, keeping the water as still as possible. When the water is quite still *float* the seaweed specimen to be mounted on to the paper and arrange it gently with a soft camel-hair paintbrush with a good point. This must be done very slowly and carefully and be sure to *float* the specimen and not dunk it right down into the water. Once you have arranged the seaweed to your liking lift the paper (with the specimen on it) *very* gently and slowly from the water. You will probably find this tricky at first, and you may have to re-immerse some of your specimens several times before getting them out still safely and attractively arranged on the paper. If the water is at all turbulent the fronds will tend to cling together as the paper is lifted out and present merely a shapeless mass on the paper. The larger and sturdier types of seaweed are, of course, easier to mount in this way but should still be handled very carefully.

Once paper and specimen are safely out of the water lay the whole thing on a sheet of blotting paper (which should have been placed as near the dish as possible), cover the specimen with a piece of cheesecloth cut to size and cover that with another sheet of blotting paper. Build up a pile of specimens in this way and then place the pile between two boards and apply *slight* pressure. Very heavy pressure will spoil some of the delicate species, but of course pressure can be increased for more sturdy specimens. The experts advise the use of slatted boards, but any boards which are not warped or too heavy will serve the purpose. For really big and coarse specimens you can dispense with the cheese cloth, but it is absolutely essential for the preservation of the more delicate samples, as otherwise they will stick to the blotting paper or become displaced and will not press satisfactorily.

Seaweeds naturally hold a lot of moisture and the blotting paper should be changed twice the first day and then once a day for another six or seven days. The more fragile specimens will be ready in about a week, tougher species take a little longer. Never try to economise by not changing the drying paper as often as recommended. It is false economy if you value the finished appearance of your specimens.

Another tricky process which will need a little practice is to remove the cheesecloth when the specimen is ready to be taken from the press. Peel with an upward movement from the bottom of the plant, and never be in a hurry. Most of the smaller varieties will have become firmly stuck to the mounting paper, but the thicker, tougher varieties will need to be fixed firmly with narrow slips of gummed linen tape across stems and at strategic points, the less the better for appearance's sake. Some people prefer to put a little dab of colorless glue beneath the fronds to attach them to the paper instead of using tape strips, but be careful not to use too much or it will make ugly stains through the specimen.

Each seaweed specimen must, of course, be labelled and as many details as possible attached to it. To the usual ones of name, location and date should be added such information as tidal level, whether found growing—and on what type of rock face—or washed up on the beach. A reliable book on algae will help in identifying specimens accurately (see Books for Further Reading, p 124). As with other pressed-plant specimens, seaweed should be either mounted in an album or kept in an airtight box or tin, and should be protected with interleaved cellophane paper (see p 44).

There is still a great deal that even the experts have to learn about seaweeds and so every collector has the chance of one day being able to provide some new piece of information which will fit into the unfinished jig-saw of algology. This, and the additional interest given by an intelligently informed approach to what one is collecting, are the main reasons why it is so necessary to record as much detail as possible about every specimen.

SHELLS—DEAD OR ALIVE

Shells are usually picked up empty but the serious collector goes for

66

the live specimen: the most perfect shells are said to be on the living mollusc. For those who like to search for these in rock pools there is one very useful piece of equipment which is used by collectors. This is a glass-bottomed box that floats on the surface and enables one to see clearly through murky or rippled water. In America these boxes can be bought from marine supply firms, but they could be made at home. The inside must be painted matt black so as not to reflect light.

Most of your shells, however, will probably be empty when found. Even so, they need careful cleaning. First examine closely any seemingly empty shell for remains of the creature which once inhabited it, for if allowed to stay attached to the shell such remains soon rot and smell offensive; so pick out with a hat pin, a skewer, awl, crochet hook or anything of this nature, and then, taking care not to scratch the lining of the shell, scrape with a penknife to ensure that all is removed. To make it easier to remove any dead remains the shell may be placed for a short while in hot but *not* boiling water, and very fragile specimens should be put into warm water only. Any mud or algae adhering to the outside of the shell can be removed by a light brushing in soap and water or a little mild scouring powder used sparingly. If shells are encrusted with barnacles these can be removed by soaking the shell in water overnight and then tapping the barnacles *sideways*, gently, with the handle of a knife. A little light scraping with the point of the penknife will clear the white or grey rings they sometimes leave on the surface.

Shells taken alive need more time and care. Getting bivalves to open is a problem to many people, but the treatment is very simple. Just put them into water which has been boiled for a few seconds and allowed to cool. The boiling removes the oxygen from the water, so that molluscs suffocate when placed in it and after a short while their adductor muscles relax, causing their valves to part. All remains must be scooped out cleanly and the shell washed in clean soapy water. The cleaning of univalves taken alive is a little more tricky but do not be put off by thinking that it is a very messy process! It need not be. Put the shells in a saucepan of warm water and bring it to the boil. Countries where glossy shells such as cowries are plentiful, remember to heat the water very slowly and allow it to cool gradually, otherwise a sudden change in temperature will crack the shells. When the shells have cooled take them from the water and start getting out the flesh. A crochet hook is recommended by experts for this job; insert it at the siphonal canal and work it well up into the flesh before starting to pull out. As you pull, slowly turn the shell; this will have the effect of 'unscrewing' the flesh and it will come out quite easily.

It is advisable to clean the outside of a shell before removing the flesh, as the latter acts as a support to the shell; this is especially necessary with fragile specimens. Also take care to avoid pressure of any kind on the lip of the shell, as this is the weak point and on fragile specimens will shatter easily.

Sometimes shells, particularly those from tropical waters, have a deposit of lime or coral forming a skin over them. This can usually be removed by soaking the shell in a 20 per cent solution of bleach, but watch it all the time as too-long immersion can cause the colours to fade. It is possible to use acid for removing such deposits from the outside of shells, but is not recommended for the amateur unless done under the supervision of a professional member of a museum staff or someone with similar qualifications and experience. All shells which have been immersed in bleach need a very thorough washing in soapy water after being cleaned.

Once you are sure your shell (of whichever kind) is clean, wash it well in fresh running water, brushing with an old, soft toothbrush to ensure that no sand is left in crevices. Dry by dabbing with a soft cloth, or in the case of very small and delicate specimens by placing them on a sheet of blotting paper and allowing them to dry naturally.

Incidentally, if you have an empty bivalve with the two sides still hinged together (eg mussels or razor shells), do not separate them;

in fact make every effort to keep them intact.

Now you are ready to display your specimens. As with all other collections shells must be clearly labelled, and full details should be entered in a catalogue index system. It is usual to display one only of each variety but where shells come in a wealth of colours and markings a full range can be shown.

Shells look superb arranged on black velvet in a specially made cabinet, but you can construct a very presentable little cabinet of your own for small specimens by sticking matchboxes together to form a miniature chest of drawers (see recommendations for fossil display, p 59). Larger shells can be set on shelves as ornaments, but strong sunlight will fade some types so keep them in shady parts of the room. Some collectors stick their specimens to cards; however, you may damage the shells if at any time you try to remove them in order to display in some other way. Naturalists' dealers sell flat velvet-lined boxes which are intended especially for nature specimens and these are ideal for storing and showing off bivalves, although if one has a lot of them to display they do become rather a costly item.

Those who live in areas where tropical shells are found will accumulate many strange and decorative varieties. Here is an idea for showing off medium-sized shells of this kind. Buy a length of fishing net about 2yd × 1yd (this can be obtained from fishing-tackle shops or yacht suppliers, or, in some coastal resorts, in the shops which sell shells). Twine into the net by their spikes such shells as murex, scorpion and spider, and hang the whole thing on the wall, where it will look most effective. As net varies in strength and mesh, the method can be adapted for quite a range of shell sizes but is not, of course, suitable for the very large and heavy ones. I have seen a very attractive display of this type in a summerhouse.

Some people like to varnish shells with clear varnish or colorless nail lacquer. This is not necessary and it does destroy some of the natural character of the shell. Far better to give it a shine by

69

buffing it with a soft cloth or a nail buffer, taking special care if dealing with brittle specimens. Very tiny shells can be polished lightly with a soft tissue.

FINE FEATHERS

Some feather collectors specialise only in feathers from the birds of their own country, but a worldwide collection is more exciting. Try to contact collectors in other countries and exchange specimens so that you have a chance of adding colourful feathers from tropical and semi-tropical birds to your collection.

You can mount feathers either in albums or on loose cards. Either way they should be protected by cellophane—as interleaving in an album or as a cover for each card. Before mounting, they should be brushed lightly with a very soft brush— a baby's hairbrush is ideal—and any particles of foreign matter should be removed. It is essential that they should be absolutely clean, otherwise they will be attacked by parasites and ruined. Spraying or dusting with insecticide powder before mounting will give them protection. Even so, there is always a risk of infestation. An airtight box in which to store the collection is a help, and to make doubly sure keep moth balls, moth-ball flakes or paradichloride of benzene crystals in the box. If in spite of all precautions your collection *does* become infested the only cure is to fumigate it. Put the whole collection in a large wooden airtight box together with an old saucer or tin lid containing liquid carbon disulphide; cover closely and leave for at least three days. Carbon disulphide is a poison and you should wear gloves when handling it; also air the box very thoroughly in the open after fumigation of a collection.

Never stick feathers down with glue or any form of adhesive; the smallest dab of it makes them look bedraggled. Attach them to sheet or card with narrow strips of scotch tape over the quills. Large feathers may have to be kept in place with a narrow strip of *non-adhesive* paper placed across them at the top or in the middle, that strip of paper being attached with tape to the mounting paper or card. As an alternative to using scotch tape (which does tend to turn yellow after a time) you could wire your feathers to display boards, using a very thin wire (15amp fuse wire would be suitable) and fastening it neatly at the back of the board. This is not, however, satisfactory on anything other than fairly stiff card.

To add interest to the collection why not leave enough space beside each feather to stick in a picture of the bird from which it comes, such pictures being cut from magazines or copied from books? The usual method of classification is of course under species and you will certainly want an illustrated reference book about birds—it is worth investing in the most lavishly illustrated one you can afford. Labelling and cataloguing should follow the recommendations made for the collections already dealt with. The fuller your notes the more interesting your collection will be to you and your friends.

WAYS WITH WEBS AND WOOL

Spiders' webs, those ephemeral and most incredibly beautiful examples of craftsmanship in nature, can be preserved for a lifetime and more if one exercises a little extra care and patience in 'gathering' them. Cut a sheet of black matt paper (see p 14) in squares of varying sizes from about 6 × 6in; make some of the pieces really big as you are bound to encounter some large webs. Select a web which is unbroken and which is spun in such a position that you will be able to place a square of paper behind it without damaging it. But before you do this hold the aerosol can of white paint about a foot away from the web and spray gently and evenly all over it. Do *not* do this if the spider is on the web; if necessary touch it with a blade of grass to encourage it to get well out of the way before you start operations. After spraying

71

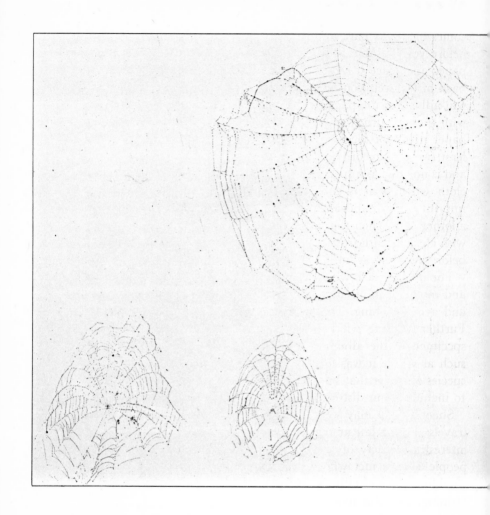

Spiders' webs

comes the tricky part, and you will probably need a little practice
before you are able to gather perfect webs. Take your square of
paper and place it *very* gently but with a firm hand against the
back of the web you have sprayed. The web, sticky with paint,
will adhere to the paper which can then be carefully withdrawn
with the web firmly imprinted on it. As the paint is still wet the
paper must not touch anything and should be left to dry for at
least two days before being handled again. If the web does break
and is no good as a specimen wipe the paper quickly with a damp
cloth when, if it is good quality paper, all traces of the web
imprint will disappear and the same paper can be used for
another try. When the paint is quite dry spray the whole thing
with clear varnish from an aerosol can and allow this to dry hard
before handling again.

For storing, each web should be covered with cellophane paper
and mounted in an album. Use one side of the album page only
and avoid rubbing. The book on spiders in the 'Suggestions for
Further Reading' will help you to identify and classify webs. Each
specimen in the album should have details written beneath it,
such as where it was found (garden, hedgerow, woods etc), the
species of spider that built it, and as many details as you are able
to include about distinctive features of the web.

Sheep's wool may sound a strange thing to collect but if one
travels about a fair amount in one's own country and abroad an
interesting variety of specimens can be assembled. The several
people I have met who have gone in for collections of sheep's
wool have all had either a farming background or an interest in
farming, and this naturally makes the subject more fascinating
for them, but any country dweller will find it attractive.

As explained in an earlier chapter the samples are taken from
tufts of wool left on prickly bushes, barbed-wire fences, gates and
so on. Each sample should be washed thoroughly as soon as you
get it home, but never use strong detergent as this will remove
the natural oil from the wool and destroy its character. Warm

water and mild soap flakes are recommended as cleansers. Each specimen when completely dry (and natural drying in the open air is best) should be mounted on a card with a dab of colorless glue. A black card is the most effective background. The label should give name of breed, origin of sample, the part of the country from which the sample comes, and any further details such as the history of the breed, particular features, etc. The cards containing samples and notes are easiest to manage if kept in a box file. Classification can be by division into short-wool and long-wool breeds, or by location: northern breeds, southern breeds, south-western breeds, and so on.

Collectors of sheep's wool usually like to visit agricultural shows to see the various breeds exhibited and often become deeply and genuinely interested in the history of breeding and the qualities of the different types of wool.

CHAPTER SEVEN

Bonsai and Fruit Trees

The Japanese word 'bonsai' means 'planted in a pot' and is said to have been derived from the Chinese words *p'en tsai*, which translate as 'a green plant grown in a pot'. A bonsai is now regarded as a miniature tree, conforming in all aspects with an ordinary tree of that species but dwarfed in size. Such trees have been cultivated for over a thousand years in Japan and for even longer in China, and in these countries there are collections of tremendous age and great value. Interest in the hobby is growing fast and there are bonsai societies in many countries; one of these, the Japan Society of London, stages a display of bonsai at the annual and world-famous Chelsea Flower Show.

Some seedling types are much more suitable than others for training into bonsai and this should be borne in mind when collecting specimens. Trees with large leaves, flowers or fruit are not good subjects, although some experts do cultivate them; for the beginner, at any rate, they should be ruled out completely. Trees with small leaves and a neat branching system are the best; some people like to specialise in species which show a fine effect of bare branches in winter, or those which show beautiful color in the autumn, but for the average beginner, just starting a collec-

75

tion from his or her own seedlings, there is more fun in growing all sorts; specialisation can always come later.

In Japan the growing of bonsai is an art and is subject to very rigid rules. Something like twenty styles of bonsai are recognised in that country and these are divided into three main groups—concerned with the shape of the trunk, with multiple trunks growing from a single root system, and with group plantings of two or more separate trees. Then there are the *mame* or miniature bonsai, the loveliest of them all, which by Japanese rules must not exceed 2in in height. These are the province of the real enthusiast, because they demand a great deal of skill and attention, and watering is so important that it has become almost an art in itself. As a general rule the larger the tree the less attention it needs, but if one is prepared to be really painstaking the growing of *mame* specimens is the great goal. The hobby is one that grows on people—to the extent that some will not even go on holiday because they will not leave their trees in anyone else's care; an old gentleman of my acquaintance turned down a free trip around the world which he won as a prize in a nationwide charity draw, simply because his bonsai would have to be taken to a friend's house while he was away, and he felt the little tree would not like being moved from its normal surroundings! But do not be put off by this—such sacrifice and devotion are not obligatory.

CONTAINERS FOR BONSAI

By tradition only Japanese or Chinese pots are used for bonsai, but these are extremely difficult to obtain and you will probably have to settle for something else. Care and thought should be given to the choosing of them and it is well worth getting really good ones. Hand-made pots are ideal and many bonsai enthusiasts make their own. If you are not a potter yourself you may know of one who would be willing to produce some suitable containers for

Bonsai: (left) *root pruning;* (right)
traditional types of pot, showing drainage holes in base

you.

Brightly coloured containers are never used for bonsai: the container must not overshadow the tree and should blend harmoniously with the type of tree it contains. A matt surface is favoured by most experts but glazed containers are just as nice, although the glazing should be on the outside of the pot only. The pots must of course have drainage holes. Why not grow your bonsai in a holed stone? These are sometimes cast up on beaches and they make most natural settings for some types of bonsai, especially firs.

Having lined up seedlings and containers, soil must be your next consideration. This is easy enough today because potting soil can be bought at any garden shop and produces good results. Japanese bonsai growers, however, would never dream of using a ready-mixed soil, but follow different soil-mixture 'recipes' for different types of tree. Even if you buy your soil ready-mixed there are a few refinements worth adding. For instance, pines (all varieties) like a rather sandy soil, and all seedlings do better with the addition of a little bonemeal to encourage growth during the early days of their existence in a pot.

TRAINING YOUR BONSAI

So you have potted your seedlings, and after about a year's growth your whole collection will be in need of serious training. Some collectors start even earlier; it depends on the rate of growth of the seedling. Root pruning is one of the secrets of successful bonsai growing, and before you embark on this it is best to read a book on the cultivation of miniature trees. This will also tell you how to train your trees into attractive shapes; how to wire, tie and weight them without cutting or disfiguring them; how to wield a sharp knife effectively, and how to give your bonsai that typical aged look. Details of three useful books are given in the list on page 134. You can put in a little extra useful practice by studying the shape of normal-sized trees of the species you are growing. This will assist you in training your miniature into a natural and pleasing shape.

Potting or re-potting is most successful if carried out in early spring, although conifers usually do better if left until late spring or early summer. Flowering trees are best repotted when they finish flowering and before the leaves open.

Watering of bonsai must be done at least once a day, and in the

78

case of strong drinkers, or in very hot weather, more than once. This is the main cause of collectors' reluctance to leave their bonsai in the care of other people, as it is so easy to forget that daily watering if you are not an enthusiast. Failure to fulfil this daily routine can prove fatal.

Quite a number of species of bonsai may be left out of doors all the year round, but remember that frost can crack pots, and so if yours are not frostproof bring them indoors. Again, if bonsai get covered in snow and the snow freezes, then the weight of it can disturb their growth—so beware of that hazard too in winter time.

ESTABLISHED TREES

If you want to add an established tree to your collection, in addition to the seedlings you are bringing on, then you can expect to get a specimen from about $7·95 up to $50·00 from a bonsai nursery; prices depend on species, age and shape. Most large greenhouses have a selection of bonsai and some carry proper bonsai pots.

If you live in or have access to hilly or mountainous country, you could consider building up your collection from established trees which have been growing in their natural habitat for a number of years and are already stunted by nature because of soil or climatic conditions. (Permission from the landowner is normally required.) In national forests, bonsai collectors may apply to forestry authorities for permission to dig certain kinds of trees in specific areas where their removal would occasion no loss, or perhaps even be beneficial. This type of collection is, however, only for the enthusiast who has plenty of room, as some of the trees may be as much as 4 or 5 feet tall when you find them and even though you will trim them down they will still need quite large pots. So if you are restricted for space it will be better to go in for *mame* bonsai or only the trees you have grown yourself from seedlings.

79

If, in your travels, you do come across a really super specimen which you just cannot leave, then be prepared for some quite hard work in dealing with it. To begin with you will not be able to pull it out of the ground or even dig it up with a trowel. The tree may have been growing where you find it for fifty years or more and have become very firmly established, so a large fork, shovel, plenty of strength and effort will be required to move it. The selection of such trees must, therefore, be done with forethought. Do not waste effort on an established tree which has not many branches but *looks* as though it may improve if you pot and look after it. It never will; if it has not grown to a good shape already, with plenty of branches, it is most unlikely to grow more, however lovingly you tend it. Similarly, waste no time over a tree which is perfect in shape and has plenty of branches but which has very large leaves or needles. It will never make a good bonsai because the leaves and needles will get bigger when the plant is cared for and fed properly.

When you find a suitable tree there is no need to cart home pounds of soil on the roots: you are going to pot it in commercial or home-mixed compost, so after digging it up shake away all the soil adhering to the roots, or gently poke it away with a stick, or wash the roots in running water. When you get it home you will have to cut out all the dead roots as well as trimming some of the rest—all of which you will learn how to do from your book on the cultivation of bonsai.

CLUBS FOR ENTHUSIASTS

If you become a real bonsai enthusiast and want to meet others who are interested in the same hobby you should join a club. The Japan Society of London, already mentioned, runs a flourishing bonsai group as part of its activities; meetings are held at which members can bring their trees for other members to see, hear lectures on the subject, and occasionally visit famous bonsai collections or a bonsai nursery. The society accepts corresponding members in other countries. There are many clubs in America and Canada, where the hobby is growing apace, as well as in other countries.

Your collection of bonsai can be handed down through many generations: the older a tree is, the more valuable it is. Some Japanese bonsai, of great age, are now worth more than $2,000 each. Bonsai, like good furniture, improve and become more beautiful with the passage of time if they are lovingly cared for. But, like all living things, they will *always* demand your attention.

INDOOR FRUIT TREES

Now, what about those fruit stones that most of us sometimes think we will plant but don't get round to? You will recall that in the first chapter I suggested that these were worth keeping as they could form a most interesting collection of indoor fruit trees; to transform a seemingly dead fruit stone into a living plant is a most satisfying process.

A heated greenhouse is the ideal aid to success, but as with all other hobbies, there are ways and means of achieving results without expensive equipment, and you can still work wonders without one. If you are going in for this hobby seriously you may care to invest in a propagating case (obtainable from garden shops), but if not, then you can start your little plants off indoors; but it is absolutely necessary that they be kept in a steady temperature of not less than 50°F or more than 75°F, if at all possible.

Gather together a number of small pots (the cartons in which cream or ice cream are sold make suitable containers) and plant one stone only in each pot. To speed germination soak hard seeds, for example those from peaches, apricots, plums and cherries, in cool but not ice-cold water for twenty-four hours before planting. Potting soil is recommended and can be obtained in small quantities from nurserymen or garden shops. If you prefer to 'do it yourself' right the way through, then you could use equal parts of sterilised garden soil, peat and sharp sand. Bulb fibre can be substituted for peat if desired. Plant each seed or stone firmly in its pot and cover it with soil of its own depth, water well and put each pot into a plastic bag, securing the top of the bag very tightly with an elastic band (make sure that the bag has no holes or splits in it). Then put the bagged pots in a dark *warm* place and forget about them for a while. The process of germinating is not a hasty one and you may have to wait several weeks before you see any sign of life.

When the first leaves appear take the pots out of the bags and put them in a warm, draft-free place in a good light but not strong sunlight. Water as necessary but do not over-water in your enthusiasm! And be sure not to put the pots anywhere where the temperature drops below 40°F. Once a fortnight feed them with a liquid fertiliser made for pot plants (Hy-Trous is suitable), following the instructions on the bottle about the amount to be used. These fertilisers are highly concentrated and too strong a solution could kill the young seedling.

As the seedling grows re-pot it. If it needs very frequent watering the chances are that it needs re-potting and this should be done immediately. Date stones are the one exception to this rule: these do better in a pot that looks too small for them and they do need a lot of moisture and warmth to germinate at all. You are likely to have more failures with dates than with anything else but if you plant a lot of stones at a time one or two of them are almost certain to germinate.

Fresh peanuts, are excellent seeds to start with as they germinate quite easily and comparatively quickly. The plants have a pretty foliage and tiny flowers. When the flowers die away the plant will start to droop; this does not mean that it is dying— far from it. The stems should be gently pressed into the soil and they will take root and form nuts where the flowers once were.

Everybody tries orange, lemon and grapefruit seeds, but you can be more adventurous and try all sorts of different things;

grapes, apricots, dates and tomatoes have all proved successful for home growing.

You may decide to be more ambitious still and propagate from cuttings—so why not start by growing a plant from a pineapple top? Slice the top off with some of the flesh still adhering and dip the cut end in rooting powder. The latter is obtainable quite cheaply at garden shops or the gardening counters of chain stores and it often produces almost miraculous results. Place the pineapple top in about one inch of really damp soil and never allow the soil to dry out. This is the main secret of success with pineapples, so they should be examined frequently. The plastic bag method is again advisable and will help considerably in getting your cuttings to root.

How long you will have to wait before your plant bears fruit varies considerably. One grower has told me that citrus fruits (oranges, lemons, grapefruits etc) do not start to bear fruit until they have been growing at least eight years, and often not for ten years; apricots and peaches also take from eight to ten years. Peanuts produce nuts after the first year, and peppers will produce fruit in one year. Pineapples take two to three years. There is, of course, always the chance that the flowers of your fruit trees may not be self-fertile and will have to be 'married', pollinated by others of the same species, before they will fruit at all. The fruits produced are unlikely to be as large and succulent as those from which the seeds came, since commercially grown fruit is subjected to many specialised processes, and usually a more favourable climate, to attain a marketable quality. But even if some of your plants do not fruit you will still have a most interesting and attractive collection, and your unusual pot plants will also make most acceptable gifts for Christmas and birthdays.

CHAPTER EIGHT

Craftwork

Some collectors do not want to arrange their finds in albums or display cases but prefer to do something creative with them. There are a great many crafts which use the kinds of materials discussed in this book, and allow plenty of scope for individual taste. Little initial skill need be required, although, of course the more adept one becomes in handling the chosen medium the more attractive, ambitious and interesting will be the items produced.

FLOWER AND PLANT PICTURES

Flowers, grasses, ferns and plant material of all kinds are popular with the collector-craftworker and can be used to make a variety of gifts or decorations for the home.

One of the simplest things to start on is a calendar, and both young people and older ones can work out their own ideas on this. Bristol board, or illustration board, bought at shops selling artists' materials, is rather splendid, but if you feel it is a little extravagant go to your local stationer and see what he can offer in heavy paper. It need not be white, a pastel-colored background gives very pleasant results, but it must be thick enough not to bend or curl. Decide on the size you want and cut accordingly.

Now spread out before you the flowers and leaves you have collected and pressed, work out your colour scheme, and select the most suitable single blooms, with sprays and leaves to go with them. Keep items for any one card in proportion. Arrange them carefully on the card, forming a spray: long pointed stems should rise up at the back of the grouping, and large flowers and leaves be set at the bottom. Trim stems to make them neat. Do not crowd the flowers but avoid too many gaps and keep the shape of the design compact. The next step is to mark lightly with pencil the position of each leaf and flower. Then take all the flowers and leaves off the card and start building up the picture again, this time permanently, because at the back of each leaf or flower you will put two or three small dabs of glue. For small, fragile items Elmer's glue is recommended; for thicker leaves or stems a stronger adhesive, such as Duco cement, will be necessary. Be sure that the glue is not in thick blobs, or when you press down your flowers it will spread out beyond them or soak through the petals and spoil the picture. As each leaf or flower is placed in its predetermined position, press it very lightly with a soft clean cloth. Try to avoid having to move anything once you have stuck it into position. To finish off the design you may like to use a long slender leaf, or a strip from such a leaf, like a piece of ribbon, twisting it into the shape of a bow to stick over the stems so that it looks as though the posy is tied. Keep a piece of the ribbon for the loop at the top of the card to hang it up by, and two short pieces for affixing the actual calendar at the bottom.

Once you have mastered the knack of arranging and fixing flowers, leaves, moss and so on, there is almost no limit to the articles which it is possible to make with them. A set of table mats would be sure to bring admiring comments from guests tired of the inevitable plastic surfaces, and so would a teapot or plant stand. For these you will need thick glass for covering; plate glass is recommended as it will withstand heat. But less ambitiously a delightful set of coasters for glasses to stand on can be made by covering with the 'synthetic glass' which is used in greenhouses and which can be bought by the yard from most garden suppliers and many do-it-yourself shops. This material is easily cut with scissors and adhesive tape can be used as a binding. Stick a piece of felt or baize, cut to size, on the base of each mat as the final operation.

For those able to cut and drill glass themselves, or with someone else at hand to do it, a coffee table would be within the bounds of possibility, using large flowers and perhaps preserved leaves rather than pressed ones. For this type of project, however, one needs to be a handyman (or woman) as well as a craftworker.

A deep tray with wickerwork sides and wooden base (the type made by blind basketworkers) can be decorated with pressed and preserved flowers and leaves. Make up the design on stiff paper or thin card cut to size and then cover it with a piece of plate glass also carefully cut to the exact measurement so that it fits snugly against the sides of the tray without slipping and spoiling the flowers.

Single petals can be used to build up complete flowers if so desired, and those who enjoy painting may like to add a background, perhaps a garden or country scene. Flowers can be arranged in such a way that they appear to be growing in the forefront of the picture. Leaves can be trimmed to size if necessary or cut into different shapes, as can large flower petals.

Some needlework shops sell brooch frames, usually oval or round, which look like midget picture frames. These are intended to hold miniature designs in embroidery, but they can also be used for tiny pressed-flower designs if you are very nimble-fingered and use only the smallest of your materials. They can be very lovely when finished and well worth the time and patience expended on them.

Then of course you can make a full-size picture entirely of pressed-plant material and can frame it yourself or have it professionally framed. It is as well not to hang such pictures in bright sunlight, as they will fade easily.

Paint spattering is another idea you may like to try, especially if you have pressed large leaves or flowers with bold clear-cut outlines. This technique is used quite often in poster and showcard work. Group your leaves and/or flowers on white or light-coloured paper or card, mix some water-colour poster paint to a thin but not watery consistency, then take an old toothbrush, dip it in the paint and with a penknife scrape up and down the bristles of the brush so that the paint spatters on to the paper. When the paint is dry lift up the leaves and flowers and there you have the plant material in outline. Alternatively, you can trace around the leaves and then, covering the rest of the paper, spatter paint inside the tracings only. Either way produces an effective and unusual picture and you will soon become proficient at it. You can experiment in adding veins to leaves and other details of this kind by masking out with paper. The same sort of effect can be achieved by spraying paint from aerosol cans. Be sure one colour is quite dry before applying another.

In the making of all types of flower pictures remember always to select a focal point, whether it be a flower or leaf; to use curved stalks to guide the eye upwards, especially if working on a long narrow piece of backing paper and to try in general to introduce curves into your design to make it interesting and easier on the eye. Don't be afraid to make long stems by joining shorter ones together, but always cover the join with a leaf, flower, bract or whatever may be suitable and natural in appearance.

It was while visiting a primary school 'open day' that I saw children making designs with seeds and realised how very effectively these, together with seed heads, can be used to create geometric designs and stylised flowers for wall hangings. Draw the outline of a design on stiff card or thin cardboard and then fill it with seeds (melon and nasturtium seeds are very suitable) sticking them on with an adhesive and using a stiletto or a cocktail stick to manoeuvre them into position. A seed head can be used for the centre of a 'flower', or can be incorporated in any design to give a three-dimensional effect.

A COLLECTOR'S COLLAGE

Whilst gathering material about flower pictures I was shown some striking collages which may appeal to those who find the ordinary 'spray' of dried plants rather dull and conventional and would prefer to experiment with abstract designs.

To start, you need a stiff backing, a piece of masonite or plywood perhaps, in whatever size you like, although it is not advisable to try fine work on a small area until you have had a little practice. The backing must be covered with coarse burlap stretched tightly and fastened securely on the underside by either pasting or sewing. Black burlap is the most effective and if you are unable to get it in your local shops you can dye a piece of natural-colored burlap in a cold-water dye. You then make up a fairly strong solution of domestic bleach and splash it on the burlap with a soft brush (eg a pastry brush). After a short while the bleach will neutralise the dye and create weird and wonderful patterns of its own accord.

When the background is completely dry you then use dried plant material, shells, driftwood, sheep's wool, feathers, even small stones, to build up abstract designs against the already abstract patterning of the background. Glue on the materials firmly, and as with ordinary dried-plant pictures do not start glueing until you are quite sure that you have positioned all the items exactly where you want them to form a pleasing collage. Strongly textured or 'bumpy' things such as shells can be stuck over flat forms, pressed ferns for instance, and the effect is really startling. It makes a magnificent wall decoration for a modern home. To

88

finish off the picture tack dowelling (obtainable from many do-it-yourself shops or shops which sell picture-framing materials) around the edge to form a·frame. In fact, it is probably better to fix the dowelling *before* you start building up your picture and immediately after the bleach has dried. This will give you a frame to work in and make it slightly easier to build up a design: and there will then be no danger of damaging the design when you start hammering in the tacks. Rings for hanging could also be fitted before work starts on the design and do make sure that these are fixed firmly and are strong enough to take the weight of the finished work.

LEAF RUBBINGS

Brass rubbings are very fashionable just now, but how about leaf rubbings? Tough, textured leaves such as ivy or fig are more suitable for this than thin or soft leaves, but after some practice you will find yourself experimenting with more tricky types and will no doubt get some very successful results with these too.

A mixture of one part India (waterproof) ink to one part glycerine is the mixture used for leaf rubbings, and this is painted over one side of the leaf until the whole surface is covered with a thin film of solution. Then take a sheet of thin, absorbent paper (rice paper is excellent if you can get it), put it over the leaf, and with the ball of your forefinger gently rub the leaf shape so that its imprint is transferred to the paper. A piece of blotting paper placed on top of the rice paper and also rubbed with the fingers will absorb excess ink solution and help to prevent a blurred outline. The prints can be mounted under glass or plastic for use as table mats, or they can be framed and hung as pictures. Vary the prints by doing some with white ink on black paper. You will find that you will probably be able to get two or three pulls off a leaf without re-inking it, although each pull will be fainter in imprint.

Making a leaf rubbing

A tough leaf can be re-inked and used over and over again and several can be grouped together to form interesting patterns. One print must, however, be completely dry before another is done on the same piece of paper, and the prints should not overlap each other or the strong outlines of the leaves are lost and the design looks messy. Do not be disappointed if your first attempts at leaf printing are unsuccessful; you will soon learn how much solution is needed to coat different leaves and which leaves produce best prints. The technique is very simple and can soon be mastered.

NOVELTIES FROM CONES

Seed pods and cones are splendid items for simple craftwork. Before starting, brush them to dislodge any particles of dirt, some may even need washing.

Birds and animals made with cones always amuse children, and large cones made into grotesque figures are 'trendy' now as ornaments about the home. Tightly closed cones and even unripe ones are best for making birds. A sitting bird has one large unopened cone for its body and a smaller one with the pointed end facing in the opposite direction for its head. Just glue the head to the body and make two feet by sticking two scales from the top (wide) end of an opened cone into position. A group of these birds of differing sizes sitting on a nest is a jolly ornament for a child—to make or to be given! Paint the cones with clear varnish to keep them from opening, and put in eyes with black paint or Indian ink; paint the pointed end of the head cone with yellow paint so that it looks like a beak. You can make standing birds by using upright cones for the body and glueing on the heads in the same way. As the cones will not stand upright on their own, use a small piece of wood (sandpapered and varnished) for a base and put a screw through from underneath into the base of the cone. Stick a small piece of felt on the underside of the base so that the screw heads will not scratch furniture. Glue in feathers for a gorgeous tail. Or paint on a white and black 'waist-coat' and you have a penguin. With pipe cleaners or wire you can make legs, horns and antennae for all sorts of cone creatures. Open cones can be hung in clusters as mobiles . . . all you have to do is use your ingenuity!

In the home of an acquaintance I recently saw a most unusual pair of cone book-ends. Four slices of well seasoned wood, about one inch thick and cut from a log, are the first requirement. Those I saw were made of ash, but oak, birch or beech are equally

Book-ends made from natural wood and large fir cones

suitable. Your local log merchant, sawmill or similar establish-
ment may be willing to cut them for you, or if you are handy
with a saw you can easily do this yourself. Log slices are sometimes
sold by florists as bases for flower arrangements, but this is a rather
expensive way of obtaining them. One end of each of the four
slices must be cut off straight, and then the slices sandpapered
thoroughly and given two coats of clear varnish. When the varnish
is quite dry place one piece of wood down flat and stand the other
piece up on it, cut end to cut end. Glue the two pieces together
firmly—Epoxy is recommended for this purpose.

On the little platform thus formed you then glue a really
large cone; those I saw were wide open but you can use closed
ones if you prefer. The base of the cone may have to be trimmed
slightly in order to make it stand up and to give a smooth surface
for glueing to the wood. When it is in position and the glue is

quite dry give the cone one coat of clear varnish. The cones on each book-end should, of course, be the same size, as must the wood slices. Two interesting pieces of matching stone, such as serpentine, could be used instead of cones, but the effect of cones with the natural wood is particularly pleasing. To ensure that the cones are really firmly fixed they could be screwed on to the wood, passing the screws up through the bottom, but—a word of warning—big cones are *very* tough to get a screw through. The bases of the book-ends must be covered with felt or baize if you use the screw method.

Another very simple way of using your big cones is to make them into cigarette dispensers. Choose really large, wide-open cones for this, and either glue or screw them to wood bases or to round cork fishing-net floats, the type with a hole in the middle that can often be picked up on the beaches. Then spray the cone with gold or silver paint from an aerosol can. When the paint is quite dry poke cigarettes in among the open scales so that they make the cone look like a prickly hedgehog. For parties, dot the cigarette cones around the room and guests can help themselves. The idea can be adapted for a children's party by lodging wrapped candy between the scales, or miniature cookies if the cones are used as a table decoration.

Unusual decorative plaques can also be made with small cones and various seed pods. Use an old gramophone record as a base—if you have none lying round at home it is often possible to buy them at jumble sales, junk shops or charity shops. The record must first of all be sprayed with paint; gold and silver are always attractive, but you can use white or a pastel color if you prefer. When the paint is dry arrange the seed pods, cones, twigs etc to form a pattern or natural display and glue them into place. You can spray these as well or leave them in their natural state. Flat rings for hanging can be glued at the side of the plaque, or one larger flat ring at the top. Epoxy is the strongest bonding agent for this job. The handyman may be able to bore a small hole through the record for the fixing of a cord, but it is a risky business as these old records are very brittle. It is safest to use wire plate-holders (obtainable at hardware shops and from some antique dealers) for hanging the plaques if you have used heavy materials for the design and if you intend them to be a more or less permanent decoration on the walls. Wooden plaques can of course be made and used for decorative mountings of this kind.

BASKETRY

Although not strictly a collecting pastime, basketry—a real old country craft—may appeal to some readers of this book. Young shoots from lilac, privet, hazel, weeping willow, even virginia creeper, ivy roots, honeysuckle, honesty, white jasmine, cat brier, and blackberry shoots can all be used for making into dainty little baskets and other articles. Bramble shoots should be left in the open air for a few days after picking, then, with a thick pair of gloves or a folded newspaper, or with a little tool sold for the purpose of stripping thorns from roses (and obtainable from many florist's shops) you can strip them of their thorns by wiping down the stems. You will need a pair of pruning shears and a sharp penknife for cutting and shaping the material, a steel knitting-needle for threading and poking the stems once you start working on the basket, a few spring clothespins for holding pieces of stem in place, and a tape measure or ruler. You can also weave rushes into basketwork or use them on their own to weave table mats, etc. Books on basketry and weaving will give you many more ideas and full details of how to go about this country craft.

POLISHING PEBBLES AND MINERALS

The most popular way of polishing pebbles and mineral specimens these days is by the tumbler method, using a small electrically-run cylinder which tosses and tumbles the stones and smooths and polishes them. But it is quite possible to polish by hand, although the method is more laborious. Smooth waterworn pebbles give the best results and these should be large enough to hold comfortably in the hand. You will require a small sheet of plate glass, a thick felt pad for the polishing stage, a sheet of thick plexyglass, and the following items which are obtainable from lapidary suppliers: silicon abrasive grit in grades 220, 320 and 500, and a polishing agent, either tin oxide or cerium oxide. The supplier will advise you on quantities if you tell him approximately what quantity of pebbles you want to polish.

The first process is sanding, and for this apply a half-teaspoonful of 220-grade abrasive grit over your piece of plate glass, moistening the grit with a little water, hold the stone you wish to polish, press it firmly on the glass and rotate it steadily, distributing grit over the entire surface of the glass, and renewing the grit if necessary. Periodically wash the stone in clean water and continue grinding until the face of the stone is smooth and free from any pits or bumps. Be very careful to keep your fingertips away from the abrasive grit and hold the stone very firmly so that it does not slip away and cause your fingers to rub through the abrasive material. It is very important to wash stone, glass and hands thoroughly after each stage of the grinding process, so after the first stage wash everything and then apply grade-320 grit to your plate glass, keeping the surface damp all the time but not too wet. Repeat the grinding action until the stone is smooth all over.

Wash again (hands, stone, glass) and take your pieces of thick plexyglass. Score the surface with coarse sandpaper, then sprinkle 500-grade grit on it and again dampen with a few drops of water. Now keep your stone completely flat on the plexyglass and continue the grinding action as before.

After this operation you will have reached the polishing stage and here you have a choice of two methods, depending on whether you want a flat 'face' only on your pebble or piece of rock or if you want to polish it all over. To polish a curved surface, that is to polish a pebble all over (and to do this successfully it must be free from cracks or holes) you will need a small glass dish with a curved interior, and the very best thing for this purpose is the type of flat jar in which fish eggs and some baby foods are sold. Moisten the jar with water and apply some 220-grade grit. Holding the pebble very firmly, use round, stroking movements to rotate the stone on the curved grinding surface of the dish or jar. Use moderate pressure; it is not necessary to apply great strength to the rotary movement. When the pebble begins to take a polish wash it, dish or jar, and hands thoroughly and apply 320-grade grit to dish or jar and continue your rotary sanding movements. When eventually it is really smooth remove it from dish/jar, wash thoroughly again and ensure that *all* traces of grit have gone from everything on your working surface. Then mix a thin paste of tin oxide or cerium oxide with water in a shallow dish, dampen slightly the pad of thick, hard felt (an old felt hat will provide a suitable material for making the pad) and apply the polishing paste to it with a soft brush. Use one or the other of the suggested polishes, but *never* mix different types of polish on the same pad.

Rub the pebble vigorously on the pad until the frictional heat which you will generate dries up the moisture on the pad and causes a slight dragging of the pebble. This is where you will need to work quite hard to get the desired effect; speed up the polishing action, lessen the pressure on the stone so that it skims the surface of the pad all the time, but keep rotating it so that the whole surface is taking the polish. Continue with this action until a good polish has resulted. Apply polishing paste as required but although it must be moist when it is applied do *not* saturate the pad, as the pebble does not start to take a polish until the pad is almost dry.

For a flat, polished 'face' on your pebble or rock do not rotate it in the final processes. As you work it on the pad, move it from side to side only but skimming the surface of the pad as in the all-over polishing action.

It is only fair to warn you that this process is laborious and takes a long time to achieve good results, so if you are anxious to get your pebbles or mineral specimens polished up with the minimum of effort you are advised to invest in a tumbler polisher. The books about lapidary work suggested in the list for further reading at the back of this volume will give you full details of this method of working.

Even if you do not polish pebbles you can still make some of your prettiest ones into simple jewellery by using them for pendants. Select smallish pebbles, preferably flat, or at any rate with one flat side. Then paint them all over with a colourless nail polish or artist's clear varnish. This will bring up the colors as when the pebble is wet. When the varnish is quite dry bind each pebble with thin copper or brass wire, leaving as much as possible of the pebble still visible and winding the wire tightly, neatly and symmetrically, so that it holds the stone quite firmly, tucking it in to secure the end. Leave a loop at the top, large enough to take a narrow silk cord or, for bigger pebbles, a leather bootlace, for hanging the pendant around the neck.

The pebble collector who does not go so much for different varieties but is just fascinated by the shapes and feel of smooth stones from the beach can display them by making pebble pictures. For these a piece of wood or masonite covered with burlap or other plain coarse woven material forms the background. The pebbles are then made to form figures and objects which build up into an amusing frieze. You will soon find that pebbles make good bodies, heads and feet; the ones with holes in can be used for heads with eyes. Once the pebbles are arranged to your liking stick them firmly to the backing with strong glue.

Another use for smooth pebbles is to turn them into hand-stones. This is a craze enjoying great popularity just at present, and is a revival of an ancient oriental custom. To relieve the tensions of life one relaxes for a few moments by turning in one's hands a smooth, cool pebble. An international magazine recently suggested that a hand-stone is the ideal Christmas present for the business executive who has everything! Choose a pebble about the size of a hen's egg; it must be smooth and nicely rounded. Then on it paint in oil colours any design you like. Geometric patterns are easy and attractive and if the stone has a hole or other natural blemish this can be made the focal point by, for instance, painting ever-widening rings round it. When the paint is quite dry go over the stone with a strong clear varnish to preserve the design.

Pebbles can also be made into amusing little figures to serve as paperweights, or even door-stops if they are large enough. A round or oval pebble can be made to stand by rubbing one end flat with coarse sandpaper; then with oil paint or waterproof ink draw large circular eyes and a small hooked beak and immediately it becomes a solemn owl! All sorts of decoration are possible from simple owls or fish to elaborate flower pictures or landscapes, according to your prowess with a paint brush. The shape of the pebble will often suggest something. When the painting is dry, several coats of clear varnish may be needed, especially for door-stops.

SAND PAINTING

Sand painting is a fascinating hobby, as well as being an excellent way of using your collected samples of different coloured sands.

The Navaho medicine men used to make sand paintings as part of their religious ceremonies: by skilfully controlling the flow of vari-colored sands from their cupped hands and through their fingers they created symbols on the ground, through which they made contact with the spirits of their gods. Sand painting could be said to have been introduced into England by George III. He employed confectioners from the Low Countries for his state banquets, and these craftsmen followed their custom of decorating the centers of the tables with sand pictures created down their full length. In Victorian times the 'painting' of sand pictures was a pleasant pastime for young ladies, and subjects often depicted were rural scenes, executed in multicolored sands. In the hands of an artist, work in sand could be very fine and hardly distinguishable from oil paintings.

To make a sand picture you need a piece of heavy cardboard, gum or other light adhesive, and a soft, well-pointed paintbrush or a cocktail stick for moving the grains of sand. First, draw a design in outline on the card. It can be a scene or a geometric pattern, in fact anything you like, but keep it simple and the areas to be covered by sand reasonably large. The whole design is then brushed with gum and when the gum is tacky then the 'painting' commences. Have saucers of different coloured sands all ready and if necessary sift them through a fine strainer. This is important; the grains must be small and no lumps of sand or pieces of grit must be allowed to remain in the 'painting' material.

Make some little pokes, or miniature dunce's caps, of fairly strong paper and glue them so that they keep their shape. Snip off the pointed ends to make holes for the sand to run through. Then using one colour at a time, and a separate paper funnel for each color, sprinkle the gummed areas of your picture with appropriately colored sands; use the paintbrush to spread the sand evenly, and ease the grains into corners or around curves with the cocktail stick. Keep the sand within the outline of the design. In 'painting' scenery it is usual for the sky to be done in water colors, but the rest of the design should be done in sand only. When the gum is quite dry, shake the picture lightly to remove any loose grains of sand and then spray it with a coat of matt-finish clear varnish to fix the picture.

DRIFTWOOD SCULPTURE AND JEWELLERY

Driftwood sculpture is not, as its name may suggest, purely the province of the gifted artist or sculptor; so often the driftwood has

Sand pictures

largely sculpted itself and only a very little trimming is needed to produce a really magnificent ornament.

It is necessary first of all to assemble a few tools. You *can* get by with just several grades of sandpaper, a sharp knife and a small saw. However, it will greatly assist in the production of fine pieces if you invest in a couple of files in different sizes, two gouges (one round, one a half-round), a wooden mallet, some woodcarvers' chisels and perhaps a rasp. Sandpaper in grades 120, 220 or 240 and 320 is essential for finishing off the work.

Before starting examine your chosen piece of wood from all angles and decide which way you wish it to stand or lie and how much trimming, if any, will be needed. You may want to alter the shape or to emphasise a hollow or curve. Then select a piece of sandpaper; the larger the piece and the harder the wood, the coarser the sandpaper you will require. Run over the wood with the sandpaper until it is perfectly smooth to the touch, finishing off with the finer grade. Rub evenly all over: not until the wood is as smooth as silk does the polishing stage begin.

It is far more satisfactory to mix your own polish than to use a commercially prepared brand. You will need one ounce of white beeswax and three fluid ounces of *pure* turpentine. Shred the beeswax into the turpentine and allow it to set; no heat is required. Teak or similar oil may be used before applying the polish to certain woods. When the polish is set and ready for use the best way of applying it is with the fingers; no other tool is so effective for working it into the wood—you get a good overall coverage and the polish penetrates the wood to a greater degree. The amount of polish needed will depend on the hardness of the wood and its absorbent properties. After rubbing in the polish leave the wood for several days before attempting to bring up a sheen with a soft cloth. Some woods may need more than one application of polish before rubbing up. This final rubbing with a soft, but not fluffy, cloth will need plenty of effort, but the finished article will prove that it was worthwhile.

101

The next stage is mounting. Some pieces will stand of their own accord and will probably look better standing free. Others will need to be fixed to a base. Obviously this also should be of wood, rubbed down and polished to match the piece of sculpture it is to hold. Heavy pieces should be screwed to the base; lighter pieces can be stuck with a very strong glue ('Heavy duty' quality is the one to go for), but screwing is far safer and rules out any risk of a sudden collapse if the bonding agent should 'give' through a rise in room temperature or other exposure to heat or to damp conditions. To keep your sculpted pieces in good trim polish them with a soft cloth from time to time; they will attain a delightful shine if this is done regularly.

Cover the base with baize or thick felt, or countersink the screw heads and fill the holes with wood filler or wood putty.

If you have collected a variety of small pieces of driftwood, worn smooth by the action of the sea, you can make 'way out' wall hangings with them. Stick them to a plywood or masonite backing, fitting them together like a mosaic. Straight pieces are ideal for this: the aim is less to derive pleasure from the beauty of the individual shapes than to enjoy the intermingling of so many different varieties and textures.

Another use for small pieces of driftwood is to make them into pendants or brooches, but here interesting shapes are desirable, and holes and indentations add interest and can also provide a setting for tiny pieces of mineral too small for display or for polishing. Do not cut your brooch or pendant from a larger piece of wood. The small bits you have found with naturally rounded edges and water-worn shaping produce far more attractive ornaments than fragments specially cut and shaped by hand. With a sharp knife or similar instrument scrape away any decayed wood and make any depressions in the wood a little deeper. Wash it well and remove any sand particles. If the wood is a nice colour and has a smooth patina it will probably be best to leave it that way, but if not it can be polished as for driftwood sculpture, varnished with a clear

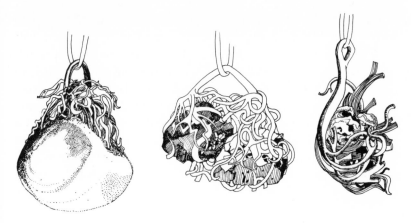

*Pendants made from dried seaweed **root** and small stones*

varnish, stained with a wood stain or sprayed with gold, silver or bronze paint from an aerosol can. That having been completed and all stain, paint and varnish quite dry, you then coat the depressions with a strong glue and into each of them drop a fragment of stone which will sit nicely in the hollow and not protrude too much from the wood. Small pieces of amethyst quartz, marcasite, green fluorite, etc, are ideal.

When the glue is hard you then bore a hole in the top (if there is no suitable hole already in the wood) through which to thread a cord for a pendant, or alternatively fix a ring at the top for this purpose. Special rings for pendants and metal brooch-mounts can be bought from craft suppliers and glued firmly to the wood. In order to effect a good bond it may be necessary first to rub down the back of the piece of wood with fine sandpaper; this of course should be done before the wood is treated in any way.

Those who are building up a good collection of shells will be unlikely to want to use their best acquisitions for any form of craft work but there are sure to be spares—those pretty shells that just could not be resisted or the ones brought back by friends from their holidays. How about the simplest of all shell-crafts—the making of

Whelk shell napkin ring

table-napkin rings? Quite often, especially on a rocky coast where shells get battered, one can find quite large shells with holes knocked right through them. Very little work is needed to make these into interesting table napkin rings. Smooth around the holes with fine sandpaper and varnish the outside of the shell with clear varnish. If the hole is not quite big enough it can be enlarged if handled gently.

Another simple idea uses shells and seaweed. Spray with paint any attractively shaped bottle and while it is still wet trail over it some olive green wool which will stick to the paint. If you have some fine dried seaweed you can trail that on instead of wool. When the paint is quite dry stick on small shells here and there, quite helter-skelter. The best effect is obtained if the bottle is sprayed in gold or silver paint, and it can be used to take a fancy candle or an interesting branch or piece of driftwood, or even be used as the base for a table lamp if a special plug socket (obtainable at lighting shops and at some chain stores) is fitted into the neck of the bottle. You could even follow up the theme by decorating the shade with small lightweight shells, perhaps using them to form 'flowers' and 'leaves'.

If you have both halves of a big clam or other bivalve you can make them into a 'butterfly' plaque to hang on the wall. Use a

104

piece of plywood as a base and cover it with a piece of strong material: burlap, or a scrap of rich velvet would be suitable. Then simply stick the shells to the base in the form of a butterfly. Antennae can be little pieces of stringy seaweed with a tiny shell or pebble stuck at each end. Small shells can be stuck around in the form of a border. Fragments of waterworn glass found on the beach could be used to decorate the shells themselves and make the 'butterfly' look more real.

Scallop shells are often used as ash trays just as they are, but they can be dressed up to make an ash tray suitable for the most elegant occasion. You will need two pieces of thin wood, plywood or heavy fiberboard, which are nailed or glued together at right angles and, if desired, varnished or painted. A scallop shell is then stuck to the flat piece of wood as the ash tray and the upright piece at the back of it is decorated with shells, seaweed, etc, stuck on to form an abstract design, or a spray of flowers—as the fancy takes you.

Shell necklaces are coming into fashion again, matching bracelets and earrings can also be made. Drilling holes in the shells is a simple matter with a tool known as an Archimedean drill, which can be bought at quite a reasonable price from many handicraft shops. The drill is simplicity itself to work and a much better proposition than knocking in holes with a nail. String the shells on nylon thread for a necklace and on strong round elastic for a bracelet. You can either knot between each shell or put a very tiny shell between two larger ones. Metal earrings and brooch mounts can be bought at many handicraft shops and the method here is to stick the shell or shells to the mount with a strong adhesive.

Shells can be built up into amusing little figures which would delight any child. A little ingenuity, strong adhesive and some paint will produce a great variety of birds, animals and people. These can be hung up if a hole is drilled in the shell at the top, or they can be made to stand on a cardboard or wooden base with

105

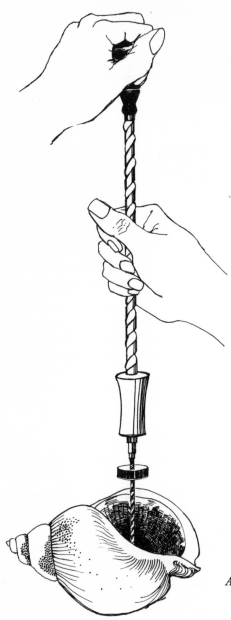

Archimedean drill

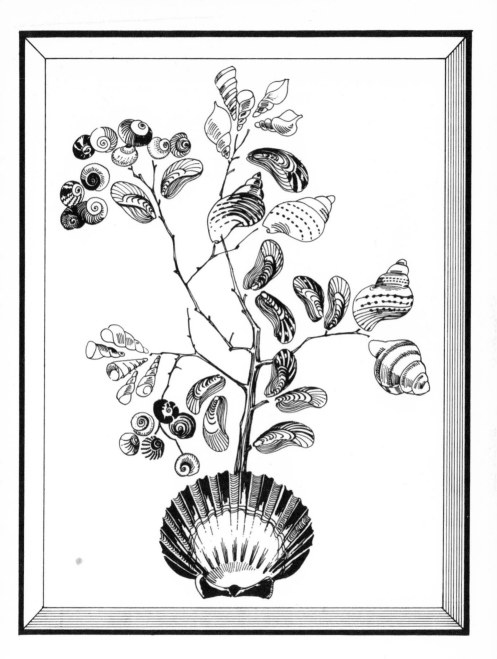

Shell flower picture

the aid of some dabs of putty, plastic wood or other filling agent.

One of the loveliest ways of using shells is to turn them into sprays of 'flowers' which can be formed to make a delightful wall hanging. This is an art in which one can become really skilled: I have seen shell pictures so beautifully done that at first glance it was impossible to spot that they were actually composed of shells. A piece of plywood or fiberboard painted matt black is effective as a backing, or use a board covered with black velvet; the latter gives a particularly rich effect. The stems of the flowers can be either slim twigs or fine wire. The spray can be built up from both large and small shells. For instance, half a razor shell at the base with half an abalone shell above it gives the appearance of a vase; from this emerges the spray with the twig forming its stem and the flowers sprouting from it. Delicate pieces of seaweed and frondy pieces of coralline can also be used to build up the spray. Slender twigs with graceful lines are most suitable, beech is perfect; thin twisted wire can also be used for stems, but this is a little more difficult to manage and should be held over until you become proficient.

Decorating boxes with shells is a form of craftwork in which the Victorians delighted and Victoriana has come into fashion again. Wooden boxes are far more satisfactory than metal ones; cigar boxes are particularly suitable. They must of course have a lid and the decoration is done on the lid only, although the sides can also be shell-covered if desired, as long as one avoids making the effect too heavy or overcrowded. The box must be clean and free of any grease and if it has been previously painted or varnished it should be rubbed down with fine sandpaper. Arrange the shells in a design which will completely cover the lid of the box; then glue them into position individually or spread a thin layer of handicraft cement or Polyfilla over the entire lid and press the shells into that. The cement should be about one-eighth of an inch thick and should not show when all the shells have been pressed into position. It is important to have the design worked out and the exact number of shells all ready, so that the work can be completed quickly before the cement starts to harden. If you are not completely covering the lid of the box but doing perhaps a central design only then it is better to use a strong adhesive such as Epoxy or model airplane cement. Keep your shells in proportion to the size of the box. When the design is finished and the adhesive or cement quite hard, the shells can be varnished with clear varnish, although I personally prefer to leave them in their natural state.

A SEASHORE PICTURE

Odd bits and pieces picked up on the beach—egg-cases of whelk, seaweed, coralline, small pebbles, bleached fragments of driftwood, etc—may not appear to be of much use once you get them home, but together they can build up most effective seashore pictures, vivid reminders of a holiday or day by the sea. Children love making these. Make the picture in a box frame with a piece of hardboard or thin plywood as the background. Box framing can be bought from many do-it-yourself or handicraft shops or from shops which undertake picture framing, but any amateur carpenter can quickly construct a suitably deep frame complete with backing.

Before making the frame prepare the background for the picture by painting it with a matt paint in white, cream or pale blue. Then work out a simple picture of beach, sea and sky on a piece of paper, deciding exactly what all your materials are going to represent and where they are going to be placed. When the paint is dry on the background you can copy your picture on to it in chalk of sort pencil and in outline only, drawing it very lightly so that any mistakes can be rubbed out. Prepare the beach in the foreground by spreading a thin film of glue and sprinkling sand on to it. Use water colours for the rest and keep the sky and sea different shades, painting in some white cloud, or, if you have a white background, leaving some of it in the shape of clouds. Keep the heavier items low down in the design and use coralline, delicate seaweed fronds and tiny shells for higher up; this will keep the picture from appearing too heavy.

IDEAS WITH FEATHERS

Feather brooches are delightful. For these you will need some buckram or fairly stiff embroidery canvas as a base, although you could use cardboard for your first efforts. On the card or canvas draw or trace the outline of a bird. Keep it very simple—perhaps a duck in flight—and select your smallest and prettiest feathers.

Trim them to fit the outline of the bird you have drawn, using perhaps a bright jay's feather or something similar for the base of the wings and so on. Align them properly to simulate a bird in flight, and when you are sure that you have a recognisable object stick them firmly to the card or canvas with colorless glue. Feathers should overlap slightly to give a gently padded effect and when the glue is quite dry you can carefully trim your bird into shape with a sharp pair of scissors if any of the feathers look straggly. It should not be necessary to trim the canvas as feathers should slightly overlap the outline. Then stick a safety pin or a special brooch pin from a handicraft shop at the back with a strong adhesive.

If you are using a canvas backing you can sew on an ordinary safety pin, but do not let stitches come through the feathers. With practice you will be able to design all sorts of bird shapes. A few small bright feathers from the jay, kingfisher or budgerigar are a very valuable addition to a collection if you are going to make brooches.

Larger feathers, including chicken feathers, are excellent for making flowers. You can also dye white feathers in cold-water dye, although you may find that some feathers will not take the dye: this is because they still have their natural oil in them. To remove this, soak them in hot water for at least twenty-four hours, then rinse in clean cold water and put on a rack to dry naturally in a warm place. The dyed feathers can be arranged on cardboard or fiberboard to form 'floral sprays' for calendars or pictures, as explained in the instructions for making dried-flower pictures, or can be made into individual flowers for decoration.

For making decorative feather flowers you start with a small quantity of plastic wood filler or some other type of cement paste. Mix a small quantity to a firm consistency, roll a little of it into a ball and then squeeze it between finger and thumb to flatten it to about the size of a shirt button. Push into this (the flower center) a thin but stout twig or a florist's stub wire. Trim feathers into petal shapes and push them into the paste before it hardens, to form the flower. A single or double daisy is the easiest flower to begin with but you will soon become sufficiently skilful to trim your feathers to petal shapes for roses and poppies. Leaves can also be cut from feathers and wired to the stems, or they can be used separately if the flowers are arranged in a container. When the paste centre is quite dry and hard, paint it to give a natural effect.

Large feathers such as the peacock's can be used for a splendid fan. Cut out the fan shape in buckram and, trimming the feathers to fit, stick them, overlapping each other, with colourless gum to both sides of the buckram. A handle can be made by smoothing a suitable piece of wood and cutting a slit in it into which the buckram should be firmly glued.

Small pheasant feathers, and also those very colourful ones shed by the jay and kingfisher, make charming little trims for hats. They are glued on to buckram or canvas and a pin sewn at the back, as for brooches. Just a spray of feathers standing up perkily is all that is needed for a hat brooch; three or four are quite enough to use in one spray.

If you are feeling very ambitious you may like to use your feathers for a complete hat. This can be as simple or ornate as you like: the very simplest design is a wide bandeau shape to go

Making feather flowers

across the top of the head, or you can buy a buckram hat-shape (obtainable from the millinery departments of many large stores, or from needlework shops) and completely cover it with feathers. Use small feathers and strip the fluffy down from them; they should also be trimmed to make them uniform in size and length. Start stitching the feathers on the hat shape at the back centre and work round and towards the crown. Stitch feathers with their spines pointing towards the crown and overlap them so that the stitching does not show—but make quite sure that the sewing is firm and that the thread goes right through the buckram shape! The hat will, of course, have to be lined and you can add trimming in the form of a small spray brooch of different feathers, or with ribbon or cord. If you are using dyed feathers, be quite certain that the dye is colourfast otherwise your beautiful hat will present a sorry spectacle after the first shower of rain! A narrow feather belt can be made in much the same way.

Feathers team very well with plant material in some flower arrangements. Pheasant feathers blend admirably in harvest designs, sea-bird feathers in marine designs, and the elegant peacock feathers can put quite a simple arrangement into the luxury class.

USES FOR SPIDERS' WEBS

Wall decorations, coasters or table mats—all welcome gifts for the home—can be made with collected webs in much the same way as with plant material. For all of them you will need stiff cardboard for backing and white electrical insulating tape (bought at electrical or hardware shops at about 75 cents per roll) for binding; for wall hangings and coasters you can use plexyglass (plastic material obtainable from garden suppliers), but for table mats you will need to use glass.

To make coasters trim the papers on which you have collected the webs to the required size and cut pieces of thick cardboard to match. Stick the web-papers to the backing cards by putting a dab of adhesive in each corner. Then cut your covering material to the same size, place it carefully on the coaster (avoid rubbing the web), and bind it round with the tape, taking special care to neaten corners.

For a set of table mats collect both large and small webs, so that you can make both dish and plate mats. Picture-framing glass is suitable for these and may be bought from a shop which does framing. The shop will cut it to size for you, although there may be a small extra charge for cutting several pieces. Be sure to supply exact measurements.

For a wall decoration or a calendar, stick a ribbon loop at the back for hanging. Glass is too heavy to hang from such a loop, so use only the synthetic material for covering any webs which you intend to use in this way.

MINIATURE GARDENS

The making of miniature gardens may not, strictly speaking, be a craft, but if you have collected seedlings and are training and growing them as bonsai, or if you are rearing plants from fruit stones, you can get double enjoyment by using them to create miniature gardens, either small enough to stand on a windowsill indoors or large enough to fill a corner in the garden or form the decoration on a patio.

Collect a few suitable containers before you start planning the actual garden. The most satisfactory container is one which has a drainage hole or in which a drainage hole can be bored. For this reason plastic bowls, dishes, trays, etc are not suitable. For indoor gardens clay bowls or clay seed pans are probably the best thing to use; if they do not have drainage holes these can be bored with a mason's drill (it may be wise to get an expert to do that little job for you, if you don't want to end up with your bowl broken into several pieces).

114

A miniature garden

For outdoor miniature gardens nothing is better than the old granite (or even weathered cement) drinking-troughs that were used for farm animals. They come in varying sizes, both oblong and round, and can occasionally be bought in auctions when farm stock and effects are being sold. Sometimes such troughs can be bought from antique dealers, especially those who include garden ornaments and furniture among their stock. Failing the acquisition of a granite trough you may be luckier in locating an old stone sink. Demolition firms sometimes advertise these for sale

115

when they are engaged in pulling down old properties; friends having alterations done in their homes may be able to provide you with one; builders sometimes have them knocking about in their yards. The town dweller, at any rate, is more likely to find a sink than a trough, though he may come across an old iron drinking-trough, a relic from the days of horse-drawn traffic. A word of warning here—granite troughs, stone sinks and iron troughs are tremendously heavy, and before buying or bidding for such a thing be sure you can transport it and get it into place in your garden. It is not possible to carry it off in a private car—it may take three or more men to lift and manoeuvre one of the larger granite troughs. Fibreglass or wooden plant containers will be perfectly satisfactory if you cannot obtain something old.

Having settled on your container and put it in a sunny position, sheltered from the wind, you must then fill it with a suitable soil. A few shovelfuls of earth dug at random from the garden or anywhere else are not likely to produce good results, sifted loam should be the basis. If it is bought from a nurseryman or one of the larger garden shops or centres, it can often be obtained already sterilised; this is a great advantage and well worth the small extra cost, as it means that no weeds will come springing up between your plants. To this loam add a half-part of *sharp* sand, a half-part of soaked peat (available in bags from garden shops; you soak it when you get it home), one part of grit and a half-part of leaf mould. This recipe has been given to me by an expert, who says it guarantees good results. But if you do not fancy your hand at mixing your own soil you can use a prepared one, sold at garden shops all ready for use, although some grit added to it will prob-ably improve it for your purpose.

You will also need to gather 'sherds'—broken china or broken pottery flowerpots. This broken material should cover the bottom of the container before it is filled with soil, as it aids drainage. Collect some stones for 'land-scaping', varying them from flat pebbles to tall, spiky ones which will simulate mountains. You are now ready to plan your garden. Place the stones here and there and find out the most pleasing arrangement of them before you start putting in your plants. Remember to bury the stones a little in the soil, so that they will look natural and will not topple over. For indoor gardens you may also like to use some miniature ornaments or figures, but do be careful not to have more accessories than plants and keep your ornaments in proportion to each other, to the size of the bowl and to the plants you have in it. A layer of grit or sharp sand over the top of the soil when all the plants are in position, and before the accessories are placed, gives a professional-looking finish.

If you make a collection of miniature gardens to be kept indoors do not stand them in full sunlight or in draughts. Although they *do* need plenty of light, right against a window can be too cold in winter and too hot in summer. And never forget to water, as necessary, both indoor and outdoor gardens.

CHAPTER NINE

Winter Work

Although outdoor collecting of bits and pieces is certainly not something which has to stop when the weather gets bad, the winter months do provide an opportunity for sorting out and improving the collection, gathering information and identifying those difficult specimens that have accumulated over the year.

YOUR LOCAL LIBRARY

At your local reference library you can use far more books than you would ever be likely to collect at home. In addition to the latest books available on any particular subject, some really old books can also be very helpful; often in their illustrations are perfect reproductions of meticulous hand drawings which show a lot more detail than even very good modern photographs. Usually reference-library volumes have to be used on the spot and cannot be taken away, but there are also plenty of books available in the ordinary non-fiction departments of the public libraries which can be borrowed and used at home. These are often simpler to use than the scientific and technical volumes. And if you are making a really good collection of plants or minerals, for instance, it is worth mastering the relevant scientific terms, one by one; it makes classification of your finds much easier.

In order to classify specimens accurately it is necessary to ascertain both their common and scientific names. In geology there is usually only one name for each mineral or rock, but in botany and palaeontology (the study of fossils) there are always two and sometimes three scientific names for each plant and animal. By careful study of the illustrations in works of reference you may, for instance, find a shell similar to but not exactly like the one you are trying to identify. You will thus be able to get the name of the family to which your shell belongs, and that will assist you towards placing it exactly.

Most reference books of the type you will need contain keys to aid classification. Some will appear rather complicated at first but a little study and some practice make the job easier. The librarian will be able to suggest suitable books and perhaps assist in explaining the use of particularly complicated keys.

MUSEUM AND UNIVERSITY DEPARTMENTS

Most smaller museums will provide local information about fossil or mineral locations, etc, and the larger ones will usually assist with identifying specimens as well and will give information concerning locations all over the world. Enquire also at your nearby university in the appropriate department (geology, botany, palaeontology) for detailed and recent information on a local and regional scale.

The Natural History section of most large museums, offer first-class information and identification service for amateurs. Ideally one should take a specimen for identification or information. It is courteous to write or telephone a museum beforehand to know if it will be convenient to bring specimens on a certain day or at a certain time, and of course essential to make an appointment with a university department. In some museums you are asked to sign a book, giving details of your enquiry, and to leave your specimen to be dealt with as soon as possible. You may be able to collect it in half an hour's time or you may have to wait a day or two—in any case, the service is free, so one must not be too demanding.

Those living a long way from a suitable museum or from a university can send specimens for identification, but there are certain rules to be observed; it is most important to write first, *before sending any specimens*, giving full details of the information you require and asking if you may submit specimens for identification. State how many you would like to send: some busy museums have to put a limit on the number they can deal with at any one time. With your preliminary letter always enclose a stamped addressed envelope for a reply.

It is a nice gesture to offer in exchange for information a duplicate of the specimen you are sending for identification, especially if it is something unusual (provided, of course, that you have a duplicate). With each specimen full details must be enclosed: where and when found (a Geographic Survey map reference should be included if possible), and as much information as you yourself have been able to discover about the object. Pack the specimen carefully in a strong container and enclose a covering letter clearly stating your name and address and the information you require, and also postage stamps to cover the cost of return postage. Then be patient—such requests for information can be numerous and cannot always receive priority.

Almost all the objects dealt with in this book are suitable for museum or university enquiries but do ensure that specimens are quite clean, mounted if necessary, and generally in good shape before proffering them for information—museums do not appreciate pieces of wet seaweed being tipped from a plastic bag on to a desk, or having to retrieve a fossil covered in sticky clay to which packing material has adhered—well, would you?

It is even more interesting, and you learn much more, if you try and identify your specimens yourself by taking them to the museum and comparing them with museum exhibits. There will always be somebody about who can help you out with information.

A NEWS-CUTTING BOOK

The compiling of a news-cutting book on your particular hobby is a worthwhile occupation which can be started and brought up to date in the winter time. You will be surprised at the number of press references which crop up from time to time on one aspect or another of your subject. Index them carefully; some of them may prove to be invaluable in the formation of your collection.

TALKING TO CLUBS AND SOCIETIES

The time when you are unable to indulge in field work can also, of course, be the opportunity to tidy and re-arrange your collection, to install new cabinets or specimen cases if you go in for these, to clean and if necessary renew your equipment and generally get it in good trim. And if you are really keen and have a nicely laid-out collection which is easily transportable you may find yourself in demand for talks on the subject to local organisations such as Women's Institutes, Townswomen's Guilds, Scouts, Guides and other groups. If you do do this sort of thing you will probably meet other enthusiasts and will undoubtedly benefit by the generosity of any number of people who remember that they have a foreign shell or stone or feather at home and want you to have it for your collection. For larger adult groups one needs to be a fairly experienced speaker. Invitations come from the groups themselves, but you can get yourself known in this field by giving your services voluntarily to the more informal groups mentioned above.

121

MARKETING CRAFTWORK

If you are going to make things with objects you have collected then the winter months will be busy ones, and if you are really proficient at your chosen craft you may try offering items for sale to a suitable local shop as Christmas approaches—or, if you live in a holiday resort or popular holiday area, in time for the summer season. Anything offered for sale must be of a very high standard, both of design and workmanship. Large stores are less often interested than small local shops, which may like to try perhaps ten or a dozen brooches, wall plaques, calendars and so on; or a local florist may agree to take two or three flourishing miniature gardens or bonsai on sale or return.

It is as well not to expect any great financial rewards; to be able to sell your goods gives added interest to making them and also encourages you to aim at a high standard of workmanship, and this is perhaps more important than the few dollars such work will—at best—bring. So make the most of the dark days and the bad weather. Tidy your collection, solve your problems, read round your subject, study your maps and plan your trips for the year ahead.

Enjoy your collections and your collecting. The items are free; take them with gratitude and consideration.

Acknowledgements

It is with pleasure that I acknowledge the help given by Mr R. H. Cory, who instructed me on the way to prepare driftwood for sculpture and how to handle it, and by my fellow members of the Plymouth Mineral & Mining Club (especially Mr Roy Shambrook), who passed on to me many of their hints for the cleaning and preservation of minerals. I am also indebted to the British Museum (Natural History) and the Geological Museum in London, for allowing me to browse among their collections of fossils, minerals and shells and for all the practical advice that they gave so willingly. To the staff of the County Library branch at Launceston, Cornwall (especially Miss V. Webber and Miss R. Cowling of the Mobile Library) I owe special thanks for their assistance and patience in obtaining for me the many volumes needed in the preparation of this book.

And finally to all my friends who share my interest in natural history in its many branches and to those of them who provided ideas for the crafts section of this book, my grateful thanks for their interest and encouragement at all times.

Books for Further Reading

Needless to say, there are libraries filled with books which refer in some way to your chosen collection. Your best references will come from the friends you will meet who share your interests. From them you will not only learn about books but also magazines and even courses which will speed you on your way to becoming an expert.

When you begin your collecting you should have the appropriate volume from one of the series of books designed to help in field identification such as:

Golden Field Guide Series (Golden Press)
Peterson Field Guide Series (Houghton Mifflin)
Putnam Nature Guides (Putnam)

There are many guides published locally which will refer to your specific section of the country. These can be found at book stores connected with National Parks and trusts, your local wildlife societies, or at stores specializing in hiking and camping.

Other titles which have been helpful to me are:

Dana, E. S. & Hurlbut, C. S. *Minerals and How to Study Them* (Wiley 3rd ed 1949)

Fenton, C. L. & Fenton, M. A. *The Fossil Book* (Doubleday 1959)

Hull, G. F. *Bonsai for Americans* (Doubleday 1967)

Ishimoto, T. *The Art of Growing Miniature Trees, Plants and Landscapes* (Crown 1956)

Ishimoto, T. *The Art of Driftwood and Dried Arrangements* (Crown 1951)

Japan Bonsai Association *The Masters' Book of Bonsai* (1968)

McDowall, P. *Pressed Flower Pictures—a Victorian Art Revived* (Scribner 1969)

Murry, S. B. *Shell Life and Shell Collecting* (Sterling 1969)

Reference books cost a great deal so it will pay you to use your local library copy until you decide which books are essential for you to have.

124

List of Suppliers

General supplier (botanical equipment, geological equipment, fossil specimens, mineral specimens):
Ward's Natural Science Est, PO Box 1712, Rochester, NY 14603
Nature-study suppliers (mainly botanical):
Turtox General Biologicals, 8200 S. Hoyne Ave, Chicago, Ill 60620
Carolina Biological Supplies, Burlington, NC 27215 and Gladstone, Ore. 97027
Central Scientific, 2600 S. Kostner Ave, Chicago, Ill 60623
Wood-carving tools (gouges, mallets, etc):
Obtain at a hobby store, artist supplier or hardware store
Bonsai:
Enquire at your nearest large florist or look in the catalogue of large mail order seedsmen such as Burpee, Field, Breck's, etc

Index

127